Game Changer Protocol

Free yourself from limiting beliefs and supercharge your life

Tim Goodenough

Copyright © 2016 by Tim Goodenough. All rights reserved. No portion of this book, except for brief review, may be reproduced, stored in a retrieval system or transmitted in any form or by any means – electronic, mechanical, photocopying, recording or otherwise – without the written permission of the author.

ISBN: 978-0-620-71536-2

Cover design: Soofeeya Tamseel
Edited by: Jo Lennox-Goodenough

Disclaimer

This book is not intended to be a substitute for the services of health care professionals. Neither the author nor publisher is responsible for any consequences incurred by those employing the methods and techniques reported herein. Any application of the material set forth in the following pages is at the reader's discretion and is his or her sole responsibility.

This book is dedicated to all those who have found a way to succeed in life in spite of themselves. Supercharging your life will open up so many possibilities and I am excited about what you are going to do and become next...

Thank you to Mike, Christof, Melonie, Danny and Barbara for your valued support and feedback. Thank you to my parents Aileen and Dave, brothers Calvin and Brendon, in-laws Elmien and Duffy, sisters-in-law Toni and Suryn, brother-in-law Erich. I appreciate and value your consistent support. Thank you to my daughter Robyn for being a source of unconditional love and for inspiring me to be a better parent who wants to make a difference in the world that you will inherit. I am especially grateful to my wife Jo. Thank you for all your support, skills and love. This book wouldn't be half of what it is without you.

Contents

One	**A wake-up call**	*- it doesn't have to be this way*
Two	**A rugged road**	*- when old school theory lets you down*
Three	**I judge myself**	*- self-esteem explained*
Four	**I'm a believer**	*- unpacking the beliefs of self-esteem*
Five	**Absolute beliefs**	*- when your 'truth' doesn't set you free*
Six	**Game Changer Protocol**	*- 10 healthy self-esteem beliefs*
Seven	**Your body speaks**	*- are you listening?*
Eight	**A solid foundation**	*- the seven principles of Scanning*
Nine	**A two-way conversation**	*- Coaching the Body*
Ten	**Aligning mind and body**	*- introducing Scanning*
Eleven	**Uncluttering the mind**	*- preparing for Scanning*
Twelve	**Step by step**	*- your very first Scan*
Thirteen	**10 weeks for 10 beliefs**	*- the self-esteem journey*
Fourteen	**Staying connected**	*- a call for community*
Fifteen	**Troubleshooting**	*- some additional support*

One: **A wake-up call**
- it doesn't have to be this way

I was desperate, angry and hurting. At 17 I was in my first real long term relationship, yet I felt hopelessly alone. Life was just too much to bear and so late one night I found myself sobbing and searching my girlfriend's kitchen cupboards for just the right knife to bring an end to it all. I was distraught, but I realised that I needed a pen and paper to write a note as I couldn't stand the thought of my girlfriend or parents blaming themselves for what I believed was my escape. However, my search of the house couldn't turn up anything to write with or a shred of paper to write on. That was the second closest I ever came to the point of no return. To this day I'm not sure if it was the lack of a pen or the lack of courage which saved my life that night.

Looking back, there was no obvious set of circumstances which could be blamed for my despair. During my formative years and the time leading up to that night I simply always felt isolated, separate and increasingly alone and worthless. I believed I was a burden to others – someone who offered little to no value.

That night was a wake-up call and when I finally reached out for help it came in the form of a psychologist and some serious meds that numbed the pain. Unfortunately the very meds that began to make my life bearable also prevented me from experiencing life in full colour. A grey fog surrounded me for four years, only lifting on occasion to allow a brief ray of sunshine through. I must have developed some resilience to the drugs because I got more pills and I got new pills, but the pain remained. I started self-medicating with alcohol and poor life choices. I lived this way for three blurry years until finally my long, slow and sometimes doubling back road away from depression and towards healthy self-esteem started with a choice.

It was another late night – around midnight on a Sunday. I was lying on my back in a muddy pool in the middle of a sports field near my university dorm. As I felt the rain pouring down on my face and soaking through my clothes I was reminded of a scene from the movie *Shawshank Redemption*. It was fitting as I was imprisoned by my own thoughts and desperate to break out. At the age of 20 I was on the verge of being kicked out of university due to poor academic results and a low class attendance record. This felt like the end of my world. I'm the youngest of three boys and my parents had sacrificed a lot to be able to send us to university. The thought of paying back that sacrifice with failure reinforced a lot of my self-hate and put me into a downward spiral. To make matters worse, after my three years of incomplete study I would now be faced with a massive amount of student loan debt and no clear way to earn enough to pay it off.

My final exams were drawing closer and my schedule was incredibly demanding as I was carrying two extra subjects after missing the prized 50% mark. To add insult to injury it seemed unlikely that I would even be allowed to write as the DP withdrawn letters were piling up (The DP certificate or Duly Performed certificate issued for each subject allows you to write your final exam based on a combination of class marks and class attendance). When the fourth DP withdrawn letter arrived the previous Friday, I realised it was game over.

To pre-empt the humiliation of getting kicked out I planned on calling my folks to tell them I couldn't do it – the pressure was too much and I was dropping out. I gave myself the weekend to find the words and the courage. My moment in the mud was an impulsive attempt to feel something other than the crushing numbness and despair that overwhelmed me when I was sober and alone with my thoughts.

As I lay in the muddy water I could hear my teeth chattering, but it took me a while to realise that I was experiencing cold and along with it feelings. Something was triggered deep within me. I had been numb for so long that I wore it like a second skin, but now for the first time I began to feel my body again. I started to experience ... something ... a feeling of being a little bit alive again. I started giggling. It was such a relief to feel something again and I embraced it. I 'owned' the madness. In that moment I made a promise to myself that I will do whatever it takes to feel fully alive again and to live the life I knew was possible. The words I used to lock that into my heart was, "Fuck it. Let's give this a full go!"

In the days that followed I begged, pleaded and charmed my DPs back. An astonished elderly accountancy lecturer remarked, 'Young man if you are willing to take an old woman like me to dinner to get your DP back, then clearly you are committed enough to pass.' I tracked down the most diligent note takers who took my classes and persuaded them to give me a break. I killed a small forest photocopying notes and embarked on a binge studying programme which saw me hitting the books hard for 15 - 20 hours per day, seven days a week for the next two months. Despite the odds I managed to pass five of my six subjects. However, the one I missed was a biggie. To pass my Computer Science major I needed 50%. There was no supplementary exam and my 44% mark meant another year of university to complete my degree. It wasn't the outcome I'd hoped for but it made me realise two things:

1) Within me lies more power to change the way I feel about myself and to positively impact my own life than in the hundreds of anti-depressant pills[1] I've taken over the years. 2) I chased an almost

---

[1] Looking back now as a professional in a related field I believe that there is a place for medication in certain circumstances. However, it should be used as a support to get your life back on track and not as a crutch to avoid dealing with your issues. I was lucky in that my cold turkey approach worked because my stubborn nature made me extra determined and I had the support of a skilled and caring community of coaches. It got me through a dangerous period. I don't recommend my style to others as there are much better ways to do it – like consulting a relevant and trusted professional.

impossible outcome and achieved 96% of that goal in spite of my fears, doubts, worries and lack of a track record. Therefore, surely much more must be possible if I had better technique and less fear?

Sixteen months later I moved to the big city. My new, yet fragile state of mind helped me to secure a place in a prestigious Merchant Banking Graduate Programme after graduation. Through a series of fortunate events I also met Anne Renew - a kind, strong and talented Neuro-Semantics Trainer and Coach. A retired architect, Anne chose her vision of empowering others over the quiet life of a retiree. She introduced me to the models, tools and mind techniques of Neuro-Semantics. It was part of her goal to teach people across Africa to 'run their own brains' – or how to exercise more choice when it came to their minds and emotions. I became part of the community which helped her to achieve that vision. The tools and techniques I learnt brought about some much needed healing and coping skills in my life. It wasn't easy, but within a year I managed to qualify as an Executive Coach and two years later I qualified as a Neuro-Semantics and NLP Trainer.[2]

---

[2] NLP or Neuro-Linguistic Programming is a practical set of psychological models, techniques and insights that can be used for personal empowerment, growth, healing, accelerated learning and a host of other benefits. Neuro-Semantics is based on NLP and is an extension of the original models.

Over the next ten years I continued my immersion in learning these new models, tools, techniques and systems and attended many coaching courses. I coached others, as well as benefited from both self-coaching and from being coached. I had a huge amount of work to do on myself, just to get to 'okay' and it became increasingly clear that one of the key areas I needed to focus on was my self-esteem.

I believe self-esteem to be one of the most misunderstood and misused terms in psychology. The face of compromised (or unhealthy) self-esteem is often thought of as depression or 'weakness'. This is not true or useful. In fact, many people who are considered dynamic and successful and are celebrated for their talents and creativity, *also* struggle with compromised self-esteem.

- Do you second guess yourself way too much?
- Do you have an internal critic that has too much power?
- Do you get anxious/stressed when things are going *right?*
- Do you worry that people are going to find out that you aren't that talented, skilled or clever?
- Do you use arrogance and bravado to feel better about yourself?
- Do you use perfectionism to drive your work ethic even if it makes life difficult for you?
- Do you make the needs of others so important that there is no space to look after your own needs?

- Do you spend too much time worrying about what people may think of you or how they may judge you?

If you've said yes to one or more of these questions you are probably one of the many talented people who have compromised self-esteem.

As someone who has searched extensively for ways to improve his own self-esteem and who continues to do so, I find it hard to relate to most of the information and guidance on offer. I have never been comfortable with the way self-esteem is described and mapped out in general by both the laymen and those in the know.

The simple definitions are jarring and the complex definitions feel complicated *about the wrong things.* A quick *Google* search will turn up about 46 000 000 articles related to self-esteem and there are thousands of books and many tips, techniques, pieces of advice and models on how to improve it. For me, too much of the advice feels like using a Band-Aid on a gaping wound. An instruction like 'love yourself' was so far removed from my reality as a young man, that it in fact made me feel worse.

With this book I provide a clear explanation of what self-esteem is and how it works. Understanding this will give you insight into how compromised self-esteem may have sabotaged you in the past and how your self-esteem can be powerfully transformed to empower you in the future.

I also explain, most importantly, how to steadily and powerfully improve self-esteem from the inside out. Healthy self-esteem has so many benefits. Your mental health will improve: you will have more energy and spend less time second guessing yourself. Your relationships will improve: You will be much better equipped to find a worthy partner, renegotiate your relationship on healthier terms or find the courage to exit a stuck/toxic relationship. Your parenting will improve: Less triggers and insecurities lead to more mature and thoughtful handling of learning moments. Your work performance will improve: Healthy self-esteem results in more confidence, performance, creativity and leadership. The energy you normally lose due to worrying about what people might think, about failure and your ability will now be focused on what you want to achieve. Your happiness will improve: There will be fewer internal triggers and negativity that holds you back and keeps you small. You will discover more openness to finding and pursuing your authentic purpose which will result in more happiness more often.

It took me 12 years of various psychological, coaching and therapy techniques and approaches to move from a place of self-loathing, to being okay with myself, to liking myself (most of the time), to embracing my uniqueness, potential and value.

Of course it doesn't have to take nearly that long. By applying what I have learnt and developed you can achieve healing and growth in months or even weeks, depending on what level you are starting from and the amount of time and the level of commitment you are willing to invest.

Whilst I was developing this model and experimenting with techniques I identified many of the challenges faced by my corporate clients and the sports teams I worked with as those which can be traced back to compromised self-esteem or more specifically: conditional or low self-esteem. As patterns of behaviour borne from compromised self-esteem became more obvious I fine-tuned the model and we applied it to their benefit.

As soon as healthy self-esteem replaced low or conditional esteem they experienced a fundamental life change. Their lives radically and rapidly improved. Seeing them flourish is what inspired me to share these tools, techniques and experiences and make the know-how easily available so that others can benefit.

I wish I had these tools and techniques when I was growing up as it would have made a massive difference. Fortunately, you can learn and implement them in your life from today and avoid many of the pitfalls I and others like me had to endure. Through my life lessons and subsequent training I am able to give you a safe, tried and tested process to develop healthy self-esteem. Why struggle or limit yourself when there are effective solutions for you to apply? Why become frustrated when there is a well-worn path for you to follow?

I believe healthy self-esteem to be the most powerful and impactful mental skill that you can develop.

It is one of the few things that can positively impact every part of your life. Think about what your compromised self-esteem has already cost or is costing you?

- Are you staying in a toxic relationship?
- Have you lost a great partner because deep down you didn't feel you deserved him or her?
- Have you chosen a safe (and boring) job and life over a life of passion and purpose?
- Are you sabotaging your own success/accomplishments?
- Are you not saying, doing or creating what your heart desires due to your fear of being judged?
- Does your need to be liked compromise who you are and what you want to achieve?
- Has the inability to say 'no' deprived you of what's important?
- Do you feel like a fraud as you desperately worry that someday someone will see beyond your mask?
- Do you lose energy and sleep second guessing yourself and worrying about what others might think?
- Has your fear of being too much like or becoming one of your parents stopped you from pursuing or becoming what you really want and embracing who you really are?

- Do you have very little or no time or energy for yourself as you consider everyone else's needs as more important than your own?
- Is fear making you stay with an abusive boss or in a dead-end job?
- Do you not ask for or keep the money you deserve as fair value for your work?
- Are you letting people treat you poorly or take advantage of you by not standing up for yourself?
- Have you given up on doing whatever it takes to realise your full potential?

What could your life be like if you fully committed to developing and maintaining healthy self-esteem?

- What could you do or become if you had enough self-belief and self-confidence?
- What could you create if you knew 100% that you could succeed and didn't give the critics/haters any energy?
- What kind of partner could you enjoy your life with if you believed yourself worthy of a great partner?
- What kind of financial health and freedom could you develop knowing the true value of what you offer?
- What kind of relationships could you develop and deepen by demanding mutual respect?
- What kind of success could you achieve if all your energy went into finding or developing your passion instead of just

using the energy which is left after the second guessing, worrying and/or anxiety?

It might be the realisation of how much compromised self-esteem has already cost you that gives you the kick in the ass you need to do something meaningful to improve your life. Or it might be the excitement of knowing you could experience life with the handbrake down that pushes you into action. You should think about both - the downside and the upside. Think about whatever gives you the most energy to make the commitment to change your life. Then do it. Change your life by committing to this book and its processes.

I know from experience that there are many people whose sense of personal value is so limited that they try to hide their true self from the world. If you are hiding from the world because you hate yourself or believe that you are weak, stupid or worthless I can tell you now – categorically: you are not weak or stupid or worthless or whatever other lie you might believe. It is your limiting beliefs which make you feel that way. You are an awesome and valuable human being and this book will help you to connect or reconnect with that truth from the inside out.

You might be thinking: '...But I do not hate myself or think I am weak. In fact my life is mostly okay if not reasonably good. Things would have gone better for me if it wasn't for a bit of bad luck, poor circumstances and the fact that some things are just not meant to be.'

Whilst that might be true from a certain perspective, just being 'okay' means that there is something missing and you most probably know you can get so much more from life. Remember, if part of you doesn't believe that you deserve more in life you will find a way to sabotage your efforts through lack of willpower, commitment, staying power or courage or any of the other subtle symptoms of self-sabotage. When people live their life believing their worth is mediocre it can be difficult to even think that it could be different. Follow and commit to the processes in this book to find out how different it can be.

This book will put you in the driver's seat. It will show you that the junk you hold in your head about yourself is limiting your quality of life, your romantic relationships, your health, your wealth, your career, your friendships and your inner peace. Negative beliefs and thoughts can be unlearned and removed – even if they are very, very, deeply held.

This book will empower you with the knowledge and techniques needed, that when combined with commitment and bravery, will kick-start and help continue your journey to healthy self-esteem. However - this is a *practitioner* book – these ideas and techniques need to be practiced to make an impact. This is a call to action. Awareness is not enough when it comes to self-esteem, you must be willing to 'go there' and to stick with the process to get the reward of living life without the handbrake up. Are you ready for the challenge?

Or do you want to spend another 10 years or more believing that your value is conditional on your achievements, on recognition, on your status, on your looks, on your position or on something outside of yourself. Take a moment to consider all that compromised self-esteem has already cost you or could cost you in the future. And then decide enough is enough. I challenge you to follow the steps in this book so that it ends today.

Two: **A rugged road**
- when old school theory lets you down

The process of developing self-worth (I use the terms self-worth, self-love and self-esteem interchangeably in this book) is very similar to embarking on a long, strenuous journey through rugged terrain.

To prepare for the road ahead the majority of books, techniques and advice available on developing self-esteem provide the novice with a backpack and a water bottle before sending them on their long journey. I will equip you with a 4x4 and teach you how to become an expert driver who can master all terrains and obstacles.

Whilst backpacking the self-esteem trail adds value and can move you in the right direction, it's a long and tough journey which spells failure for those who lack strong willpower and high levels of motivation. People with poor self-esteem will tend to also criticise themselves when progress is slow and will therefore be more likely to quit. Low self-esteem reinforces low self-esteem and it's especially tough to 'backpack' your way out of that vicious cycle.

Commonly accepted 'backpacking' advice on how to improve self-esteem include:

- Improve your self-talk i.e. say nicer things to yourself.
- Fake it until you make it - act like someone with healthy self-esteem and visualise it until it becomes true.
- Use your body[3] to positively influence your mind's chemistry. (When you hold specific strong body positions such as the 'Wonder Woman' pose for as little as two minutes there is proven benefit)
- Focus daily on appreciation and gratitude.
- Stop comparing yourself to others and stop judging yourself and others.
- Stop criticising yourself and mentally beating yourself up.
- Exercise!
- Don't try to be perfect. Celebrate small steps forward.
- Develop self-compassion – treat yourself like a best friend as often as possible (rather than being your biggest critic).

So why is this 'backpacking' and what does '4x4-ing' look like?

'Backpacking' advice is primarily aimed at the conscious mind and requires a reaction. It means you are required to react to a negative

---

[3] Amy Cuddy, a Social Psychologist and Associate Professor at Harvard Business School, is a pioneer in this area. Her TED-Talk, *Your body language shapes who you are* and her 2016 book *Presence: Bringing your boldest self to your biggest challenges* explain some of the most powerful conscious methods to shift your chemistry.

situation or thought with a positive counter suggestion or solution by using the conscious mind.

Here are two examples of using this approach:

As a 22-year-old I achieved one of my life goals by attending a seven day NLP Practitioner Training. I had spent eight years thinking on and off about how interesting and valuable the course might be whilst planning my future trip to Santa Cruz which for many years was the only place you could attend this training. Much to my delight I discovered that I could attend this same training in South Africa. Through fortuitous circumstances I got my chance and when the day finally came to attend the training I was full of excitement. However, because of my low self-esteem, I found myself unable to ask any of the burning questions I had in the classroom as I was deeply afraid I might waste the others' time and be rejected by the group.

My solution was to machine gun questions at the trainer, Anne Renew, at every break. This worked for me, however she often wouldn't get any tea or lunch because of my harassment. She gave me the advice to be kinder to myself and to stop judging what might happen. Great advice, but very hard for me to action. During class when I wanted to ask a question, my negative judgement would immediately kick in and I would fight it in my head with weak positive words and awkward attempts to say kind things to myself with my internal voice, 'You are not so bad' and 'It might work out less horrible than you think.' It took me another six days of training to work up the courage to ask my first question in the group. (Have you ever had that experience, where you had value to add or a burning question to ask however you swallowed it because at some level you felt you were not good enough or that you will be judged harshly?) I stuttered my question and felt my face burning with shame even though the question appeared to add value to others. I had temporarily conquered my low self-esteem induced fear and over the next few months I slowly improved in this area.

Whilst using willpower helped me, I would not have been able to make the progress I did without some of the techniques I was learning. The style of using conscious willpower alone to try bring about change is also a fairly common approach when people are trying to lose weight. I'm sure many can relate to my friend Angela's story.

Angela normally feels terribly low and 'fat' after weighing herself on the bathroom scale. One Monday morning, however, instead of her usual negative response she had committed herself to respond in a new and more positive way. She had read a self-help article about the benefits of self-compassion and knew she was sadly lacking in this area. She wanted to try to not be so tough on herself and began to focus on the three kilograms she recently lost rather than the 10 she had to go. Monday was a good day for her and she had the emotional energy to start to count the positive steps forward. She even said to herself: 'Maybe it's not so bad?'

This shallow high lasted for about four minutes until she saw her profile in the bathroom mirror. This triggered her body image shame and she started to tear up. She wondered if she could ever get out of this cycle as this 'positive thinking crap' doesn't work for her.

Although it can and sometimes does shift thinking, this type of willpower driven approach requires a lot of awareness and discipline to yield results and is an extremely slow process. This approach is based on the theory that if you feed your conscious mind enough 'good stuff' it will influence and improve your (significantly more powerful) unconscious mind over time. Whilst these methods have made a positive difference to some super committed people, they have more often been the cause of great frustration and negativity to the majority who can't see it through, fail and are then too discouraged to try again.

Bruce Lipton, a former Stanford University Researcher and the author of *Biology of belief,* estimates that the conscious mind processes information at about 40 bits of data per second whereas the unconscious mind operates at about 40 million bits of data per second. Self-esteem is stored in the unconscious mind. It can be *influenced* by the conscious mind through determined and consistent work. However, you can also access and change self-esteem by tapping directly into the unconscious mind. Therefore – it stands to reason that you'd choose to gain access to the part of your mind that is millions of times more powerful than the other part. I call the technique which allows us to work directly with the part of the unconscious mind where self-esteem is stored, *Scanning*. Later in this book I will share with you the step-by-step process of how to use *Scanning* to unlock your healthy self-esteem.

Once you've mastered this new technique you will be firmly in the driver's seat of your 4x4 with both hands on the wheel, negotiating the rugged terrain towards healthy self-esteem with much more ease.

The journey towards mastering *Scanning* involves sufficient understanding of the thinking and theory behind all its core elements followed by focused practise. Over the next few chapters I will share those important elements with you. You will have the choice to learn the bare minimum to be effective or to delve deeper into the theory and research that holds it all together. The choice will be yours to learn at the level that is best for you.

Understanding self-worth (a.k.a. self-esteem, self-love)
The dictionary defines self-worth as 'the sense of one's own value or worth as a person.' So, in order to develop self-worth it is important to understand how that 'sense' or self-evaluation process works. In what way do we evaluate ourselves? Where do we store that evaluation? If we understand *how* self-esteem is created and stored in the mind, it goes a long way towards revealing how to fast-track its development.

Therefore my definition of self-esteem differs slightly from the dictionary as I believe we need to include more detail on *how* self-esteem is created.

Self-esteem is your overall personal judgement of your own value. It is not a logical judgement.

It is also not just one judgement, but rather a series of judgements which when combined create a distinct way of experiencing and interpreting life - which in turn can affect every part of our daily lives.

These judgements influence our romantic relationships, friendships, parenting styles, health, wealth, careers, spirituality, overall performance, general happiness and more.

All aspects of your life are influenced by your assessment of your personal value.

These personal judgements sit both in the conscious and unconscious mind. Some moments that lead to personal judgements are easy to recall and others are harder to pinpoint. However, it's not necessary to remember the precise moment in time when a younger you made a personal judgement, which affected your sense of self-worth, for the effect to have an impact on you as an adult.

People often do not expect low self-esteem from those who, on the outside, appear to have it all: good health, many talents, a successful career, a healthy bank balance, a loving partner, lots of friends and an attractive face and body to boot. However, even those who appear to have it all can feel worthless or not good enough when they judge themselves on the inside.

World renowned celebrity Angelina Jolie, who was once voted the sexiest woman in the world by a leading men's magazine, is a good example of this and has been quoted as saying:

"I struggle with low self-esteem all the time! I think everyone does. I have so much wrong with me, it's unbelievable!"

These judgements of value that create self-worth are formed primarily during our formative or younger years and may even include your birth experience[4]. Experiencing trauma during this period and even later on in life, is likely to (but not always) result in toxic negative judgements about things that are linked to the trauma and about yourself. 'I am unlovable.' 'It's all my fault.' 'I am broken.' 'I am not safe.' 'There's

---

[4] Sharon King in her excellent book, *Heal your birth, Heal your life* explains her powerful process to mentally heal yourself from any trauma during the birth experience. Birth trauma can create negative judgements about one's self and/or the world. Her process clears that trauma and those judgements to bring about healing which can have a significant and life-changing impact on your adult self.

something wrong with me.' 'My needs are not important.' 'I will be abandoned by others.' Whilst this book is not focused on healing major trauma, these techniques can be used with your therapist, coach or councillor to deepen the level of safety and support that is often needed to work through major trauma. Instead this book is focused on helping those high functioning adults that have built a level of success in life in spite of some of their limiting judgements about themselves. As such it is important to understand how these judgements are formed.

The example set by parents and/or caregivers and the lessons learnt from them are very often at the heart of judgements created early in life. Even loving and well-meaning parents can contribute greatly to their children developing poor personal judgements and a sense of not being worthy.

In order to help identify the origins of judgements formed during childhood, I've outlined a few scenarios which can impact self-worth – you might be able to recall similar experiences from when you were growing up.

1. Jane is throwing *the* temper tantrum of her short life in the middle of the local grocery store – much to the dismay of her mother, who responds with: 'Girls who get angry and scream like that are naughty and will get punished!' It's an understandable parental response, however, according to Jane's young mind she is not allowed to and/or it's not safe to feel emotions like anger. (A better parental response

would be: 'It's okay to feel angry, however hitting mommy or screaming like that is not okay.')

2. Young Yusuf doesn't want to disappoint his father, so much so that he does whatever his father tells him to, which includes following a maths and engineering path. The problem is that Yusuf is actually highly artistic and creative and feels dulled and limited by maths. However, Yusuf is too scared to say 'no' to his father and continues to do what he thinks will please him most.

3. Ten-year-old Thabo is very proud of himself for scoring top marks in his math test and shows off his gold star to anyone and everyone. His dad congratulates him, but also worries that Thabo might become arrogant. He gives the youngster a tough lecture on not being, "too big for your boots." Thabo learns that being arrogant is wrong and that being proud of yourself means you are arrogant.

4. Samantha blurts out the wrong answer to a simple question in class. All the kids burst out laughing and she even hears the remark, "I can't believe she's so stupid!" The teacher just shakes her head and clearly thinks it's funny too. At that moment Samantha's internal critic is given a job for life, 'Keep quiet to keep safe.' (As she grows older that voice is never dialled down or switched off.)

5. 'Children should be seen and not heard'. That's the belief of Bongani's parents and therefore they do not consult with their kids about issues concerning them. Instead of being asked questions, Bongani always only gets told what to do. He therefore concludes that he doesn't matter and that he isn't valuable enough to be asked for an opinion.

6. Zack is very allergic to a variety of foods and needs to have special meals. When the other kids swop sandwiches during break time at school or there's birthday cake in class, he cannot participate due to his restricted diet. Zack stands out when all he wants to do is blend in. He comes to the conclusion he doesn't belong.

7. Karen has two older brothers who excel at sport and they enjoy the passionate support of their dad in particular. Karen's passion is playing the violin – something her dad doesn't understand or enjoy. It feels to her that her brothers can easily make their dad proud as long as they play sports. However, when it comes to her violin - even though Karen practices for hours on end – her dad's muted support and lack of interest means to her that she is not enough to make him proud.

8. When it comes to changing a plug or a car tyre or tinkering with a broken appliance – Jack's dad is the man for the job. The teenager always watches in amazement how his dad

fixes everything, wishing he could do the same. But whenever Jack tries to help out, his efforts go unnoticed and unsupported. His dad will immediately take over the fixing or repairing as soon as Jack hesitates or does something wrong. Jack does not try to help that often anymore. He doesn't experience the trust and support he needs and concludes that he does not have what it takes.

9. 'Thunder thighs.' That's the refrain Clarissa hears in her head when she looks at her legs. She knows this to be true as their neighbour's son once saw her in a swimming costume and screamed, "Thunder thighs!" at the top of his lungs. She then concluded that her life will be completely different - if only her legs looked different. Only then would she accept herself.

10. Twelve-year-old Jacques is very smart and his family is already talking about him becoming a doctor one day. Jacques's mom, a perfectionist, often shares with him how successful she could have been if she herself was pushed harder. So when Jacques brings home a 92% mark the conversation is focused on what went wrong with the 8%. When he gets chosen as a school junior prefect[5] and not junior head prefect his mom can't hide her displeasure and

---

[5] In South Africa many of our schools have an elected leadership group amongst the senior scholars – this leadership group is called prefects.

tells him that this might very well affect his future. The constant feedback about his many 'failures' creates fear and insecurity in Jacques who now believes he isn't good enough no matter what he does.

11. Johnny knows that his football coach has a temper and does not take any prisoners. He tries to do everything right to escape his wrath. Despite Johnny's best efforts he one day gets called out and shouted at by Coach for being "a dumb ass". Worse than that – Coach tells the team that Johnny cost them the game. For him it's a foregone conclusion 'I am stupid! I am useless! I am an idiot! I am going nowhere in life!' The shame is too much for him and so he emotionally checks out of giving his all and doesn't enjoy football anymore.

If you are reading this book you can probably relate to some of the stories above and have your own similar story to tell. Sometimes the story is different, but the judgement is the same. 'I am not worthy' 'I am not good enough.' 'I can't accept myself.' 'I don't matter'...

What childhood judgements are you still carrying around with you?

Unfortunately, for most people, the personal judgements made as a child when determining personal value are very likely to remain in place as the judgements of the adult. Even though these judgements are out of date, or not logical - or both, they have a very real impact on the adult's day to day life, hampering future happiness. Seldom are these judgements naturally overcome or 'outgrown', regardless of whatever level of success or love you experience as an adult.

An adult who is navigating life with the distorted and negative judgements of a child continues to be limited by and held back by those judgements.

Many of the examples below won't be considered self-esteem problems by those living with these judgements as they would just consider it to be the way life is.

1. As an adult Jane finds it extremely hard to deal with emotions like anger, frustration or disappointment. She frequently experiences bouts of depression because her younger self never developed a healthy relationship with these emotions. All Jane knows is that it's bad to feel angry and it's wrong to feel disappointment. She doesn't *do* confrontation. It's not okay when those emotions *happen to her*. She is terrified of being promoted to a managerial position as then her job would require her to have tough conversations and deal with anger and frustration, which she just *can't* do.

2. Because Yusuf never managed to stand up to his father he now struggles with saying no - when that's what he really wants to tell others. He finds it hard to set and hold healthy boundaries. He often steps in to do what his work colleagues are supposed to and slaves away at the office when others have gone home long ago. Yusuf still believes he has to please people for them to like him and he can't say no to their requests (whether these requests are reasonable or not.) He genuinely feels that he doesn't have choices in some key areas of his life.

3. Forty-year-old Thabo is so focused on being humble that he undersells, underplays and hides his true abilities, skills and personality. He doesn't take credit for any achievement, not even in his own mind. At work he has been passed up for promotion twice because he comes across as lacking confidence and self-belief. It doesn't help that he stumbles and stutters when asked about his work or that he refers to his accomplishments as 'nothing much'. This style erodes his confidence and self-belief. He is so focused on never being arrogant that he can't see himself accurately and fairly.

4. By now Samantha is so used to hearing the harsh words of her internal critic that she can't remember a time when the critic wasn't in charge of her life. The internal critic demands that she holds back, keeps a low profile and plays

it safe. She is constantly worried about what people might think or say about her. She knows they will judge her and even label her in a negative way. She is constantly exhausted from second and triple guessing herself and playing through worst case scenarios in her mind.

5. Due to his parents' style of parenting Bongani now struggles to make his own needs, wants and desires a priority as deep down he believes he doesn't matter. He often gets taken advantage of by takers[6] and runs the risk of being burnt out by their needs replacing his needs. (These takers can be friends, family, work colleagues or all of the above.) In Bongani's case it seems that his life is centred on his wife's career, needs, interests and friends.

6. Even though his food allergies are a thing of the past, Zack the adult still feels like an outsider. He tries hard to fit in at work and socially, but due to his insecurities his efforts quickly backfire. At work he brags about his achievements and abilities, which leaves him isolated. On a social level he is needy when meeting and interacting with girls and he

---

[6] Adam Grants' book, *Give and Take* is an excellent resource for understanding the dynamics of giving and taking. It gives insight into how to prevent burnout as a giver and explains that as a giver you need to draw boundaries for takers as takers won't draw those boundaries for you.

quickly finds himself in the dreaded 'friend zone.' He hopes an achievement, accolade, acknowledgement or a pretty girlfriend will give him a sense of belonging. (It doesn't. Belonging is an inside job.)

7. Karen gave up playing the violin years ago. She didn't see the point in further pursuing this passion as she never got the support from her sport-mad dad or brothers she so desperately wanted. She also believes that it does not matter how hard she works or whatever success she achieves as she will never be enough and certainly never as good or as loved as her siblings. Every Christmas and family gathering she hopes that her dad will pull her aside and show her the same love he shows her brothers to heal the hole in her heart. It hasn't happened yet and the stress and resentment is steadily building.

8. Many years have passed since Jack lived under the same roof as his father, but the old man still makes his son feel inadequate for not being good with his hands. As a kid, Jack concluded that he cannot solve problems and so his mature self is hesitant to take on challenges. He ends up making excuses when great opportunities present themselves. Jack simply and firmly believes that he doesn't have what it takes. Around the home his wife has become the handyman and she teases him about it. Even though he

pretends to find her remarks funny, he is hurt by the teasing and it makes him feel like less of a man.

9. Whilst Clarissa has found general happiness as an adult, this quickly turns to misery as soon as she picks up a few extra kilograms. Even as an adult it's difficult for her to fully accept herself unless her strict, unrealistic and of course unnecessary conditions for acceptance are met. She avoids photos and dreads birthdays - as both remind her that she is losing her self-worth with every passing birthday and extra kilo. Clarissa doesn't realise that she is teaching her daughters that same style as the example of her behaviour is stronger than any positive words she parents with.

10. Jacques only made it to his second year of medical school before dropping out, which caused a major rift in his family. His parents believe that he had betrayed his gifts and let them down. For Jacques the truth is that he could no longer bear the pressure of delivering top marks all the time, when his best often wasn't good enough for his parents. He found medical school depressing. In fact he felt depressed overall and needed to escape. Jacques now does odd jobs to get by, whilst maintaining a steady diet of beer. He doesn't really see or speak to his parents anymore as it just stirs up too much pain and

disappointment for all of them.

11. The shame he experienced as a child still has an impact on Johnny as an adult. He clearly remembers how it felt to be belittled by his football coach and ridiculed by his peers. Deep down he believes that he isn't worthy of connection, love or belonging and as such he keeps choosing girlfriends who treat him badly and crush his spirit. His friends don't understand why he is so unlucky in love as most people will consider him to be 'a catch'. Johnny however seems to only feel comfortable in an unhealthy relationship. Whenever he dates a nice girl it feels like something is 'missing.' (He doesn't realise that what he is unconsciously missing is the drama and pain he can't picture a relationship to be without.)

Negative judgements can create a set of symptoms which include self-criticism, fear, insecurity, stress, anxiety and more. An adult can often clearly see how others are limited by their own illogical judgements, whilst failing to recognise the same in themselves. Adults can be blinded by their own childhood judgements.

An adult living with multiple negative judgements about themselves can get so used to the fear and anxiety that it feels normal. Normal that is, right up to the point where things go very, very badly for them and they experience a life crisis. A failed relationship, a health scare, a frightening bout of depression, getting fired, screwing up at work, being passed up for a major promotion or a family rift may be the catalyst needed to seek ways to improve their self-esteem.

The problems that are created from unhealthy childhood judgements can persist for long periods of time and sometimes even a lifetime. Eventually people get to a place of believing, 'that's just the way it is' or 'that's how life works' or 'it's always been that way.' The truth is that it doesn't have to be. These judgements can be changed, if you are equipped with the know-how and willing to do the work.

I will share with you the step-by-step process to steadily and powerfully replace unhealthy childhood judgements with healthy adult beliefs that will empower you, uplift you and change you. It will be your game changer – if you commit to doing the work.

Three: I judge myself
- self-esteem explained

In the world of psychology there is no single unifying understanding of or explanation for self-esteem. What does exist is a wide range of definitions, descriptions and levels to explain it. What helped kick-start my understanding of self-esteem was the Neuro-Semantics distinction that describes the difference between self-esteem and self-confidence and introduced me to the concept of the difference between *being* and *doing*.

Self-esteem - is the sum total of your personal judgements on which you base your value as a *human being - who you are*. It is a value which is therefore not attributed to anything that you offer, contribute or achieve. Self-esteem is most commonly referred to in terms of either high or low, but other terms used to describe levels of self-esteem include middle, global, domain-specific, compromised, healthy and conditional.

Self-confidence - is directly linked to your *human doing - what you do*. It is your automatic and personal assessment of the likelihood of success (good or bad) - given a specific situation and/or task. Said slightly differently: self-confidence is the automatic answer to a subconscious and situational question, 'How likely am I to be successful here?' The answer arrives in the form of a feeling – and this can range from high to low self-confidence.

Self-confidence is a very useful and practical personal skill. It's important to be aware of your own likelihood of success when considering any given task. This for instance prevents us from doing dangerous and foolish things in the first place. It also informs us when more preparation or practice is needed. For instance, just because you never miss an episode of the medical TV shows *House* or *Grey's Anatomy* it does not mean you are capable of diagnosing illness or performing surgery on a friend.

Furthermore, self-confidence is directly influenced by self-esteem. Someone with healthy self-esteem can assess their level of self-confidence more accurately versus someone who has low self-esteem. When you are living with low self-esteem the automatic self-confidence question changes which makes it much harder to feel and keep the same level of confidence as someone living with healthy self-esteem. In short, low self-esteem restricts confidence.

For instance, whilst many people can effortlessly and passionately share their ideas with family and friends when gathered around the dinner table, few will be able to do so for a TED talk taking place on stage and in front of hundreds of strangers.

So why does this happen? Why can someone who is physically able to do a talk or deliver a speech and even be good at it, not do so given all circumstances? Where does the skill go? Quite simply – as soon as the thought of a negative outcome starts to dominate the thinking, the skill is forced to take a backseat to feelings like anxiety and fear. Will they laugh at me? Will they jeer? What if I forget what to say? What if they don't like me? What if they think I am stupid? The negative impact of these confidence-draining thoughts is multiplied when combined with low self-esteem.

When I am approached by clients wishing to work on what they call their low self-confidence, I've learned to first check their level of self-esteem. More often than not it is their self-esteem which needs work and we first need to shift their personal value judgements, which make up their self-esteem, in order to build their confidence.

Where in your life have you experienced low or reduced confidence when logically you shouldn't have as you were capable and skilled enough to be successful? Asked differently, where in your life has compromised self-esteem derailed your performance?

The three categories of self-esteem

As I've stated previously, self-esteem is commonly categorised as high and low. However, through my research, work and life experience, I have come to the conclusion that a more useful and accurate term for describing 'high' self-esteem is healthy self-esteem. To fully map out all the relevant dimensions of self-esteem a third level or category must be added, namely conditional self-esteem.

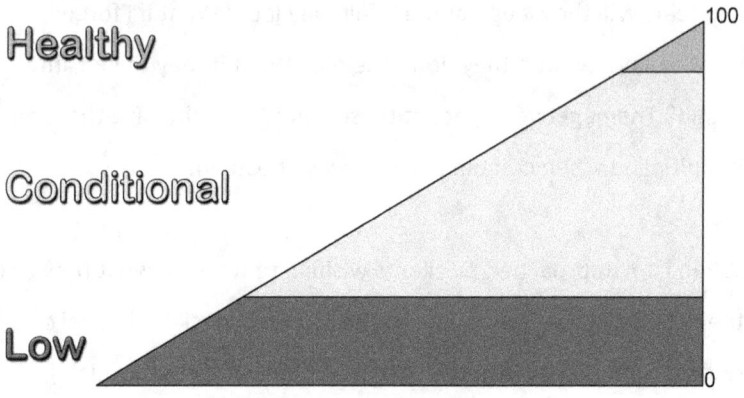

1. **Low self-esteem**

   People with low self-esteem wake up in the morning with a very low sense of personal value. If this was indicated on a hundred-point scale (with 100 being the best and 0 being the worst) their score would be close to 0/100. They may hold one or a combination of beliefs such as, I am not okay, I don't matter, I don't belong, I am not enough, I don't have what it takes, I am not worthy, I am not accepted, I am not good enough, I am not lovable - or variations of the same themes with different words such as - I am worthless, I am horrible, I am no-one, I am nothing, I am a waste of space, I am disgusting, I am pathetic, I am weak, I am stupid. These deeply held beliefs can have a range of different outcomes including low-confidence, passive-aggressive behaviour, self-hate and self-disgust.

   Those with low self-esteem often keep a low profile, stay quiet and try to remain invisible. They generally want to mask what is going on. They tend to hide. Sometimes it means hiding within a group through conforming, or hiding behind a happy façade by sporting a big smile and always agreeing with others. Their self-talk is typically negative, overpowering and highly critical and they often feel too embarrassed to share it with others. They find it difficult to accept compliments and negative thoughts can quickly spiral out of control. There is likely to be high levels of anxiety, fear and shame.

Whilst anxiety and fear are worthy of discussion in relation to self-esteem, it is shame which I believe can be the most devastating and which calls for deeper analyses. Shame is the "intensely painful feeling that we are unworthy of love and belonging" as defined by shame and vulnerability researcher Dr Brené Brown.[7] She says shame is one of the most primitive human emotions we all feel and the one no-one wants to talk about, even though it can destroy lives.

When people live with shame they often act out against themselves and the results include depression, eating

---

[7] Dr Brené Brown is a Research Professor at the University of Houston Graduate College of Social Work. Her excellent and inspiring 2010 TEDx Houston talk, *The Power of Vulnerability*, was a key influence in how I approached my research as were her powerful books *Daring Greatly*, *The Gifts of Imperfection* and *Rising Strong*.

disorders, alcohol, drug or steroid abuse, pervasive negativity, addictions, anxiety and other related conditions.

Brown explains that it's important to understand the difference between shame and guilt. Whilst shame is a focus on self, guilt is a focus on behaviour. In other words, shame is personal. It's focused on the human being, not feeling worthy as a person ('I am such a failure', rather than 'I failed'). Guilt is focused on the human doing, therefore feeling bad about certain behaviour or actions ('I'm not a loser, but that was a loser idea'). Guilt can be a useful and positive emotion as it can imply that someone wants to be better and owns that they can be. Guilt can therefore be a call to corrective action. Shame, however is destructive and not effective as a tool to correct behaviour.

Shame can be easily created when harsh judgements are made by a parent, teacher, friend or even your inner critic: You are useless! You are a horrible person! You are a loser! You are a bad boy! You are a waste of space! You are a liar! You are a disgrace! You are worthless! (A note to parents – there's nothing wrong with confronting a child about lying, but calling a child a liar, rather than calling out that they lied, can create a label and become a self-fulfilling prophecy.)

Brown's research shows that in a prison population, the most dangerous people are those prone to experiencing shame, rather than guilt.

2. **Conditional self-esteem**

    People who have conditional self-esteem wake up in the morning with a sense of personal value, which is conditional on external factors such as their reputation, status, job, achievements, cars, money, relationships, looks, weight, body, skills, net-worth and/or a combination of the above. I am okay because I have a good job, I am accepted because I am thin, I am worthy because of my good reputation, I am enough because I make good money.

    Their self-esteem can also be attached to factors which are harder to measure such as: being better than others, being liked, being right, being perfect, being smart, being needed, being the centre of attention, being in control, being admired, being validated, being praised, being cool, pleasing others, etc. It may even be linked to a partner's validation, status, looks or behaviour. Some parents even attach their self-esteem to the behaviour and achievements of their children.

    Arrogance (also known as having a big ego) is a common form of conditional self-esteem. Arrogance can be defined as, 'an unhealthy belief in one's own importance.' An arrogant person experiences their conditional value through comparison, whether it is accurate or not. Their focus is to be better than, more than, superior to others far beyond any reasonable level of value. Arrogant people mentally and emotionally 'push other people down' with their language and actions to elevate themselves. Because people with conditional self-esteem link their value to things on the outside, they are likely to instinctively defend or protect that value, sometimes aggressively, sometimes passively. Here are a few examples of conditional self-esteem:

Carmen and her boss Lucy are not seeing eye-to-eye on the new staff policy Lucy is determined to implement at work. All the feedback Carmen, as head of Human Resources, has received from the workers point to the fact that the new policy will be ineffective and bad for morale. However, every time Carmen tries to bring it up she gets shut down by her boss, who has even called her "disrespectful" and "not a team player." Carmen concludes two things, that it's better not to speak up and that her boss is an ass. The reality is that Lucy's personal value is attached to her work and she experiences any criticism of her policy as direct criticism of her.

Mark is a very successful trader. He buys himself a fancy new car every few years and makes a point of placing his key-chain in clear view at social gatherings. He likes to talk about his successful deals and how much money he makes. It's important to him that people know that he is successful. Mark seeks out and sometimes even receives validation for his fancy car and his exaggerated stories. In those moments he feels like he is enough and that he belongs. When people respond to his bragging with contempt or withdrawal he simply puts it down to them being jealous or inferior.

It's never nice to lose, but for Clyde, the sports manager of a big league football team, a loss is a painful personal experience. His conditional self-esteem means his team's performance is tied directly to his own value. At a press conference following a beating by their arch rivals, Clyde is questioned about his team's 'losing streak' and his own commitment is called into question. Whilst Clyde is not known as an aggressive man to his friends, family and colleagues, this is enough for him to fly off the handle. His 'ranting' incident even becomes a YouTube hit!

Sports coaches and managers often tie their own value to their team's performance and the rollercoaster of emotions that follow from the inevitable losses can lead to tirades, moodiness, depression and health challenges. The reality of sport is that any time two teams face each other, 50% of the people involved lose.

People with conditional self-esteem often respond to negative feedback with aggression, sulking or withdrawal. Conditional self-esteem can also prevent people from taking risks. They often choose to rather play it safe and to stick with what they know and are good at, as they fear being 'exposed': I am not going to try that, I will look like an idiot! When conditional self-esteem includes the need to be liked, people tend to compromise themselves by making easy short-term decisions, with a negative long-term effect. For business leaders both the fear of being exposed and the need to be liked can cause them to avoid tough conversations and decisions. Should a parent be driven by the need to be liked their parental style will certainly lack discipline.

2.1 The language of conditional self-esteem:

Conditional self-esteem can be divided into three sub-categories: high, medium or low.

High: almost always
'Yes, I am certain of my value, unless: I lose my high profile job.'
Medium: sometimes
'Yes, I know I have value if/when: I can maintain my goal weight.'
Low: almost never

'No, I don't feel valuable unless: I get praise from my boss.'

For some people certain types of conditional self-esteem can be especially hard to change due to its benefits. When your value is linked to conditions like being perfect, feeling good enough, feeling acceptance or belonging (and other conditional self-esteem variations) it can be a powerful driving force behind your work ethic. The thought of replacing these conditional self-esteem beliefs with healthy self-esteem beliefs can create a fear of losing what makes you successful. Do you fear that if you lose your conditional self-esteem beliefs you may lose your success or what made you successful?

What makes changing this style even more challenging is that the benefits are often very unconscious. When I ask clients the question, 'What are the benefits that your style gives you?' the answer is normally, 'What?! Nothing, it just makes me miserable.' However, when they slow the question down and reflect on it, they very often discover powerful benefits that they haven't worked out how to get elsewhere.

Ask yourself, 'What benefit am I getting from having this conditional belief?' This answer will take some time to emerge, so keep this question in mind and wait patiently for what message you receive. The follow-up question to reflect on and experiment with is, 'Where or how else can I receive this benefit in a healthy way?'

3. **Healthy self-esteem**

   People with healthy self-esteem wake up in the morning with an innate sense of their worth: I am enough. They have a deep sense of equality, belonging, self-acceptance and self-efficacy[8] which is combined with a strong sense of their personal power. How that shows up in the world is through more authenticity, humility, creativity, accountability and vulnerability. Due to their strong sense of worth and the ability to see value in others, people with healthy self-esteem are more likely to have healthy interpersonal boundaries.

   They tend to not do things to prove themselves as there is no need. Instead their actions are more often aligned with their values and purpose. If this was indicated on a hundred-point scale (with 100 being the best and 0 being the worst) their score would be nearer to 80 or more out of 100. It is a bit of a philosophical, but relevant, question to ask, 'Is 100 even attainable?' Maybe. Maybe not. If it's really important to you to get to 100, my guess is that you

---

[8] Self-efficacy is the positive belief someone has in their ability to learn how to do, become or handle something new.

may have a perfectionist style of thinking. This style is often associated with conditional esteem and your number may be lower than you feel comfortable with, and that's okay. Wherever you are on the scale, once you can own it you can move it.

It's important to note that healthy self-esteem is not a fixed state of being. Even people with healthy self-esteem can from time to time discover that they've attached conditions to their personal value. Life happens. However, what is common amongst people with healthy self-esteem is that they are more willing to reflect and do the work to adjust their thinking and mindset in order to reclaim their internal value and delink it from conditions.

Self-judgements are held in the mind in the form of beliefs.

To better understand the origin of self-esteem, or what creates self-esteem, it is important to note that the judgements we make about our value, (at any given time but generally during our formative years) remain in our unconscious mind in the form of beliefs. People with low self-esteem have made primarily negative childhood judgements that have resulted in negative beliefs about their value. People with conditional self-esteem have made primarily positive childhood judgements which have conditions or rules to maintain or activate them. People with healthy self-esteem have made primarily positive childhood judgements or have updated their childhood judgements; the result of which is healthy beliefs about their value that don't have any conditions attached.

I believe that in any given community at any given time you will find only a fraction of people who live with healthy self-esteem, whilst the vast majority will live with conditional self-esteem. In my experience, those with low self-esteem are often experts at hiding their debilitating mindset and their numbers are therefore much larger than what we'd like to think.

So what are the benefits of understanding the three categories of self-esteem and being able to identify the general behaviour of those who fall into each category?

I believe that being able to identify your own mindset (or the mindset of a loved-one) and where you fit into the equation is of great benefit as you take the first steps towards healthy self-esteem. This book will help you to move up the triangle toward healthy esteem, no matter where you may find yourself at this very moment.

Four: **I'm a believer**
- unpacking the beliefs of self-esteem

One of the key breakthroughs I made whilst researching self-esteem was the realisation that self-esteem cannot be considered to be one thing. It is the combined effect of a number of things: judgements. These judgements stay with us in the form of beliefs.

So, if self-esteem is the combined effect of a number of beliefs, we need to ask the questions:

- How many beliefs?
- What is the nature of those beliefs?

For example, if self-esteem is the combined effect of 10 specific beliefs and those 10 beliefs are healthy and unconditional, the combined output will be healthy self-esteem. By the same token, if the 10 beliefs have conditions attached to them the combined output will be conditional esteem. If the beliefs are unhealthy or toxic, they combine to create low self-esteem.

Examples

Healthy: I fully accept myself no matter what.

Conditional: I accept myself when I am slim, but not when I pick up weight.

Unhealthy: I cannot accept myself – there is too much about me I can't stand.

Healthy: I am good enough. It is not up for debate.

Conditional: I am good enough when my dad or my boss validate me. (On the rare occasions I do get praise from them I feel good enough for a short time.)

Unhealthy: I am not good enough and can't imagine feeling that way. I try, but nothing I do changes this.

Healthy: I belong. In any group, in any team, in any context and in every room I walk into. (Even if I am in the minority and regardless of any outside politics.)

Conditional: I belong if there are a few people like me in the team/class that I can spend time with and/or the group's leader is consistently engaging with me.

Unhealthy: I don't belong, not by a long shot. My mood shifts between being worried that I'll get found out and feeling like I am a complete outsider and unwelcome. I feel like a fraud.

Not all beliefs are created equal. Beliefs are held at various levels of power in your mind. Imagine your mind being a New York City skyscraper with every floor holding beliefs about all sorts of things. Beliefs held on different floors are often linked[9]. The higher up you

---

[9] The Meta-States model developed by Dr L. Michael Hall is a key model of Neuro-Semantics. The model describes how we can have beliefs about our beliefs and even those beliefs can have many more layers of beliefs linked to them.

go, the more powerful the beliefs are. The beliefs that reside at the top of the skyscraper, where the CEO suite is normally situated, have power over the beliefs at lower levels. This mimics how a CEO and his/her executive team influence the entire company. When a CEO level belief changes, all the beliefs that are linked to that CEO level belief change too. This is the heart of the Meta-Coaching methodology[10]– how to find and shift the relevant CEO belief(s) to unlock the new mindset someone needs to combine with action to achieve their specific goals. The *Scanning* technique I will share with you later in the book can shift beliefs all the way up to the CEO level.

It can be the case that one person has eight unconditional healthy beliefs and two toxic beliefs, which means that overall he or she is closer to healthy self-esteem than its alternatives. However, certain situations, events or scenarios can still trigger the two toxic beliefs to poison the mind, despite the fact that the toxic beliefs are outnumbered by healthy beliefs. If this happens it is likely that these toxic beliefs are at a higher level of the mind than the other healthy beliefs.

The triggers that will activate toxic beliefs are often what most consider to be major life events like losing a job, going through a

---

[10] Meta-Coaching is the core coaching methodology I was trained in and still informs much of my coaching approach. Meta-Coaching was co-developed by Dr L. Michael Hall and Michelle Duval.

divorce, or losing a loved one. Toxic belief triggers, however, can also be things which might only seem to be a big deal to the person experiencing it: weight gain, criticism, a break-up, an injury for an athlete, a smaller than expected bonus at work, not doing something perfectly, etc.

When the toxic belief is activated the person with generally healthy self-esteem may exhibit many of the same symptoms and behaviours as someone with low self-esteem. This may include experiencing the nagging of a negative internal voice, trying to mask what is going on and feeling various negative emotions.

My friend Angela, who was struggling with her weight and this 'positive thinking crap', used to think of herself as having rock solid self-esteem. She had great confidence, charisma and fierce self-belief and was often at the heart of social gatherings. She has many positive childhood judgements and prided herself on having low emotional baggage. That is until she put on some extra weight that she couldn't easily lose, even when she followed the diets that worked for her in her youth. Once it became clear that the extra weight was not budging her self-belief and self-confidence plummeted. When she tipped the scale at a certain weight it was almost like her childhood judgements turned to the negative. Why? Her negative CEO beliefs about her weight was more powerful than her positive childhood judgements. This lead to a cycle of negativity, self-criticism and judgement. It required a change of attitude, 100% commitment and some intense work to release so she could return to the more genuine version of herself.

The school of Ontological Coaching asks a great question about the toxic beliefs or negative judgements we hold about ourselves: 'Do you believe you were born that way? (With that limiting or negative belief about yourself?)' For the majority the answer is a clear – 'no!'

It therefore stands to reason that if you weren't born that way, you must have learnt these limiting or negative beliefs somewhere along the way, which means you can unlearn them! What an empowering thought.

Five: **Absolute beliefs**
- *when your 'truth' doesn't set you free*

The beliefs that combine to create healthy self-esteem are different kinds of beliefs. Firstly, they reside at the CEO or the highest and most powerful level of our mind. Secondly, they are absolute or unconditional beliefs, as a belief which is not absolute is by definition conditional and would therefore contribute to conditional self-esteem. Thirdly, these specific healthy beliefs are healthy in every circumstance and situation.

This may sound obvious, but it is important to understand that beliefs can be healthy in some circumstances and unhealthy in others. For example, believing it is 'critical to focus on finding mistakes' is the kind of belief I want the safety officer checking the airplane before I fly to have. However, if that safety officer took the same style home to her husband their marriage could soon be under severe pressure...

As such absolute beliefs need careful consideration before adoption. The majority of absolute beliefs are limiting in some way, shape or form. These include extremes like fanaticism, intolerance, dogmatism, racism, prejudice and toxic absolute beliefs linked to low self-esteem, as well as more everyday limited thinking like stereo-typing, generalising and classifying often complex situations to be either black or white - leaving no room for grey areas.

Some examples:

'Those who don't belong to my religion are inferior to me.'

'All foreigners/vegans/liberals/pacifists are ..... '

'Poor people are stupid.'

'You are either with us or against us.'

'I must be available to my kids at all times, and therefore I cannot pursue my own interests.'

'I am not really a good person, and I live in fear every day that people will find out.'

'My partner often tells me I'm stupid, but I deserve it because I am not a good wife/husband.'

Absolute beliefs linked to values or moral codes serve as important guidelines and often inform our distinction between what's right and what's wrong. However, it can get challenging, confusing and/or stressful when absolute beliefs are applied to a scenario which cannot be classified as black or white, but falls within one of the many shades of grey life presents. For example, a wife who still carries a bit of extra weight after the birth of their baby asks her husband: 'Honey, do I look fat in these pants?' or an insecure child with a lisp asks her father: 'Daddy will the kids at school notice that I am different?' Can you imagine the hurt it would cause if the husband and father valued extreme honesty over compassion and relationship?

The world and life are filled with shades of grey and when we falsely simplify a shade of grey into a black and white answer there is normally some cost.

Absolute beliefs that create or imply a comparison can also be limiting.

When absolute beliefs are linked to a comparison that may not always be true there's a risk of creating a fixed mindset[11] which can be very limiting. For example, 'I am talented', 'I am a winner', 'I am the best.' These sound like positive beliefs to hold, however, when that belief gets challenged by an experience in the real world which undermines that belief (someone else is clearly more talented than you, you lose, you are no longer the best) the wheels can come off for certain types of individuals. To avoid that, carefully chosen absolute beliefs must focus on our being - who we are, instead of our doing (what we do). They must not include any comparison and they must be healthy for us in every scenario and situation.

---

[11] Carol Dweck's insightful book, *Mindset* describes the difference between the fixed and growth mindset and the significant difference these two types of styles present for anyone at any stage of their life. Having a growth mindset means believing you are a work in progress and that you can work towards becoming smarter or better at anything. A fixed mindset is the belief that talent, ability, skills, any characteristic or attribute that you have is locked in at a certain level: 'I cannot improve those things that are fixed, it is just the way it is.'

The *Four Point Healthy Absolute Belief Check* can determine whether a belief is healthy or not.

Ask yourself:
1. Is it focused on my being? (Instead of my doing.)
2. Is it focused on me alone? (Instead of comparing myself to others.)
3. Is there any scenario where having this absolute belief may be unhealthy or costly?[12]
4. Am I happy to believe this for the rest of my life, all the time and everywhere?[13]

Healthy self-esteem = a collection of specific healthy absolute beliefs.

What specific beliefs and how many beliefs need to combine to create healthy self-esteem? To assist with answering that question as accurately as possible I applied a high-level principle and a concept: *The Goldilocks Principle* and the concept of *The Minimum Effective Dose*.

---

[12] This is based on the NLP Ecology question which checks the overall health of a decision: 'Is it positive for me in every way that counts?'

[13] This is the ecology test again, asked in a slightly different way.

The Goldilocks Principle

I am applying the *Goldilocks Principle* to this work so that it is 'just right' for anyone committed to seeking growth and powerful solutions. The *Goldilocks Principle*, named after the children's story *Goldilocks and the Three Bears*, refers to the porridge Goldilocks chose in the story. It was not too hot and not too cold, but comfortably in the middle.

When a book is 'too light weight' and filled with shallow yet well-meaning advice about change, it might help to challenge you to think differently, but will lack proper instructions on how to reliably do so. When a book is 'too complicated and heavy', it leaves only academics and professionals in the field able to fully understand and get through it.

The Minimum Effective Dose

Tim Ferriss in his book *The 4- hour body* speaks about the quest for *The Minimum Effective Dose* when it comes to fast-tracking growth. He asks: 'What is the smallest possible dose that will produce a desired outcome?' Throughout my research into self–esteem I kept asking the questions: 'What is the minimum amount of healthy beliefs required to be installed as absolutes in order to create healthy self-esteem?' and 'Exactly what are those healthy beliefs?' There are a few reasons why a minimum amount of healthy beliefs is important. The first reason is that a large number of people experience similar challenges during their formative years and share the same self-judgements as a result. Of course people also report unique experiences which produced less common self-judgements and beliefs. Instead of mapping out and sharing all the alternatives and variations that exist, which may not be relevant to the majority, I focus on the healthy beliefs that are consistently universal.

This leads me to the second reason - the *Pareto Principle*. Named after economist Vilfredo Pareto, the *Pareto Principle* states that for many phenomena, 20% of invested input is responsible for 80% of the results obtained. Explained another way, 80% of consequences stem from 20% of the causes. This principle has been found to be relevant across a variety of different areas, genres and topics. For example, in business 80% of a company's revenue tends to come from 20% of its customers. I've identified 10 specific beliefs that I named the *Game Changer Protocol.* These beliefs are the 20% invested input I belief is needed for developing 80% of healthy self-esteem.

The third reason for focusing on a minimum amount of healthy beliefs is to lessen the chance of overwhelm. Working to improve self-esteem can be both exciting and challenging. There is no need to over complicate the process and to proclaim a need for 19 beliefs, when 10 can be all that is needed.

So what are these 10 healthy absolute beliefs?

Six: **Game Changer Protocol**
- 10 healthy self-esteem beliefs

After a rigorous process, I have identified and arranged into order the 10 most relevant, impactful and powerful beliefs that are at the heart of healthy self-esteem. I call the collection of 10 beliefs the *Game Changer Protocol*. It's the result of my research, my training, my experience with my clients and my own self-coaching. The order is important as some of the later beliefs build upon the earlier beliefs and the early beliefs are typically small enough to not make the steps to healthy self-esteem feel too overwhelming.

Key influencers in my research include Brené Brown, David R. Hamilton, Dr L. Michael Hall and Craig Wilkinson. I also discovered that many of these 10 healthy beliefs and phrases appear again and again in multiple books, talks and papers related to self-esteem. Many of these beliefs have also spontaneously emerged as the missing solution during numerous coaching sessions with clients as well as from my own self-coaching and active reflection process. As such it is often difficult to pinpoint one person as the source of an empowering belief. The exception to this is Brené Brown's wonderful phrase which you find later on in this chapter, "I am worthy of love, connection and belonging."

As you read through the following list do an internal check with each belief: 'Right now, is every part of me saying 100% 'Yes' to this belief? Or do I have conditions such as 'Yes unless' or 'Yes when 'or

'Yes if' or 'No unless.' Or do I have an outright 'No'?

The 10 Healthy Beliefs of the *Game Changer Protocol*:

1. **I am okay.** This means experiencing a sense of inner peace, feeling fine, being alright and at ease. Being okay is the logical opposite of being in the fight or flight state: the state of stress and/or fear which causes a change in your body chemistry to prime you to fight or run for your life.

2. **I take full responsibility for what is mine and let go of what is not.** Taking responsibly is an often misunderstood phrase. What it does mean is: 'I fully acknowledge, own and have choice over all my beliefs, thoughts, emotions, words and behaviours (even the parts I don't like about myself) – including my internal voice. I take full responsibility for what is mine and let go of what is not mine.' (This statement is adapted from the *Power Zone* technique.[14])

---

[14] The *Power Zone* is the name of a Neuro-Semantics technique where you focus on amplifying a sense of ownership about something that is important to you. You then transfer the feeling of that ownership to what you think, feel, say and do. The original *Power Zone* technique was created by Dr L.Michael Hall and there is version of the original pattern in **APPENDIX A.**

3. **I matter.** People who struggle with low self-esteem often hold the limiting belief of 'I don't matter.' The opposite empowering belief – 'I matter[15]' adds value on multiple levels. It implies value. 'I have value therefore I am not worthless'. It also implies a level of significance, without implying arrogance. (The fear of being arrogant often leads to people overcompensating and putting themselves down.)

4. **I belong.** Feelings of not belonging are often a large barrier to performance and being real, and I've seen this many times in sports teams. It's also important to feel a sense of belonging as part of a family, community, business, country and the world. This belief is especially important during transitions such as a new job, new role and new environment. When you feel excluded it causes anxiety and you are more likely to act out of fear.

5. **I am enough.** Believing that you are enough is a key belief to reducing or even removing overly critical self-judgement. When this healthy belief combines with 'I belong' and 'I have what it takes' it reduces the 'feeling of

---

[15] Hearing Craig Wilkinson's powerful TED talk, *Real man, real dad* and reading his valuable book *Dad: The Power and Beauty of authentic fatherhood* reinforced the importance of believing 'I matter' and another core belief 'I have what it takes.'

phoniness in people who believe that they are not intelligent, capable or creative despite evidence of high achievement'[16] also known as 'The Imposter Syndrome'. The healthy belief 'I am enough' is also an important foundational piece for positive body image.

6. **I have what it takes**. This belief is key to achieving self-efficacy: the positive belief someone has in their ability to learn how to do, become or handle something new. As such this belief not only speaks to having a deep level of resourcefulness, it also speaks to a deep sense of resilience.

7. **I fully accept all of myself**. To fully accept oneself it is important to understand that acceptance is about empowerment. It is not about being passive, giving in, abdicating or surrendering to the role of a victim. It means that I accept the current reality of how I think and feel about myself. 'I fully accept myself just the way I am so that I no longer give any energy to self- criticism or negativity about myself. Instead I can use all that energy to focus on what I want to become and how I want to experience my life.'

---

[16] The Imposter Syndrome is a term coined in 1978 by Clinical Psychologists Dr Pauline R. Clance and Suzanne A. Imes.

8. **I am good enough.** I don't need to compare myself to others because I know I am good enough, regardless of what others can or can't do, have or don't have, achieve or don't achieve. My way of doing something, expressing something, creating something is good enough. Whilst the belief 'I am good enough' and 'I am enough' might feel the same to some, others view the two as vastly different. Feeling and believing that you are not good enough is a common self-judgement for children of perfectionists or overly critical parents.

    Another common category of people who lack this belief is children who grew up in dysfunctional homes. A child notices that when he or she does something well or are successful at something (for a few moments) that family dysfunction is paused and instead there is a happiness in the household. When the family's drama is the focus of attention again, rather than the child's success or efforts, the child very often starts to blame him or herself. 'If I was just good enough, Dad wouldn't get so mad all the time.' Or 'It's because I am not good enough that Mom drinks so much.'

9. **I am a work in progress.** (a.k.a. I grow and learn in all aspects of life). This is Carol Dweck's growth mindset in action: 'I believe that all my abilities, even my most basic ones, can be developed and improved, even if it might take

me some time. The more I work at something the smarter and better I get at it.'

10. **I am worthy of connection, love and belonging.** This is the heart of Brené Brown's living wholeheartedly concept. To live wholeheartedly means to be willing to 'let go of who you think you should be, in order to be who you are.' These beliefs of worthiness support you fully experiencing connection, love and belonging so that you don't question yourself by saying things like, 'Who am I to have this?', 'One day my partner will wake up to the fact that I am not as amazing as she/he thinks.', 'Unless I do or have X then I don't deserve this.' Or sometimes simply, 'I don't deserve this.' Instead you are able to more easily appreciate, value and be grateful for all the wonderful connection(s), love and belonging you have in your life and be fully open to receiving even more.

Those who do not feel worthy of love and belonging are often crippled by feelings of shame. Believing that you are worthy of love and belonging lessens the frequency of feelings of shame, whilst improving our ability to deal with shame itself more effectively.

In Chapter Twelve I show you how to internalise each belief, one at a time, so that you have a strong, deep and confident 'Yes' about each one. You will learn how to remove and work through any objections to these beliefs regardless of whether you are living with low self-esteem, conditional self-esteem or just want to strengthen and reinforce your healthy self-esteem. However, first it is important to understand how beliefs live not only in the mind, but in the body too.

***Game Changer Protocol* Assessment**

The table on the following page lists the *10 Beliefs of the Game Changer Protocol.* For each belief tick the box that most applies to you right now and then calculate your score based on which boxes you have ticked. Each box has a score, e.g. 'Yes 100%' is 10, 'Yes unless' is 8, both 'Yes if' and 'Yes when' score 5, etc. Work out your *Game Changer* score out of a possible 100.

Game Changer Protocol - 10 healthy self-esteem beliefs

	No	No unless	Yes if/when	Yes unless	Yes 100%
	0	2	5	8	10
I'm okay					
I take full responsibility for what is mine					
I matter					
I belong					
I am enough					
I have what it takes					
I fully accept all of myself					
I am good enough					
I am a work in progress					
I am worthy of connection, love and belonging					

My Game Changer score: _____ /100.   Date:

Seven: **Your body speaks**
- are you listening?

Over the last 12 years I have immersed myself in the world of High Performance Sport, working with both individuals and teams. I've been fortunate to have been involved in a variety of sports and at multiple levels, from school level to semi-pro to the elite level, with both men and women and with athletes and coaches around the world.

Early on in my career it became clear that whenever I partnered with a dynamic coach who focused on developing a strong culture, we were able to jump categories in performance: moving from the bottom of the league to the middle, from the middle to the top quadrant, from non-playoffs to playoffs. Teams who normally lost in the final won the trophy, teams who before only dreamt of making it to the semi-final or knockout stage of a competition or league started to compete at that level. They achieved their PBs or personal bests as a team. (It has to be said that I have also worked with teams who did not experience this category jump, but it wasn't very often and those lessons were learnt and incorporated into the formula for the next team project.)

Over time my business partner Mike Cooper and I fine-tuned a system to fast-track this category jumping. We enjoyed this work and were part of some great successes, but also sensed that something was missing and that the teams we worked with should be able to achieve even more. We knew that another level of growth existed, but only understood fragments of it, whilst the bigger picture remained unclear.

As part of my process to find this and other answers (and to kick-start my life again after a really tough 2010) I began to challenge myself in ways I never before imagined possible. I deliberately stepped out of my comfort zone intent on using my mental coaching skillset to find my way back to a happier place, whilst solving some of the frustrating performance questions that plagued me. I was my own guinea pig.

What followed was a series of sometimes risky, often cheesy and silly, but always uncomfortable scenarios. In 2010 I free dived with sharks, jumped off a tall building and a stadium, got my ear pierced and bleached my hair (to look like MacGyver for a fancy dress party). The hair and earring caused a few uncomfortable moments in corporate boardrooms and 'serious' meetings. I also entered a competition which posed the challenge: 'What is the most daring thing you can do in your speedo?'

Every uncomfortable situation I created and experienced brought hidden anxieties, fears and limiting beliefs to the surface. I always knew that they were there and that they were holding me back. At the time, this was the only way I could see to get them front and centre. (When you are surrounded by 30 sharks, 5km from shore, wearing nothing more than a tiny speedo, it creates a whole new level of awareness around fear.... and truth.)

Not only did I create uncomfortable experiences for myself, I also embraced them when they presented themselves. In 2011 I participated in a local dance show, *The Celebrity Dance-off* which is similar in format to the ballroom dancing reality show *Strictly Come Dancing*. Up until then my ballroom dancing experience was limited to a few awkward group lessons as a 14-year-old in preparation for a school dance.

My talented and patient dance partner showed me the ropes and we practiced to a level where we could compete. I had to employ all my mental preparation skills before I finally felt ready to perform in front of an audience and a panel of judges. It was important to me to do well as I wanted to do our hard work justice (and not look like a fool on the dance floor of course). When I heard the first notes of our routine's song on competition night I stole a glance at the judges and saw expressions of great expectation. Immediately my legs started to wobble and my torso turned stiff as a board. I couldn't understand it. Mentally I was armed to the teeth, ready to tackle every nerve wrecking moment. However, when I had to perform, every muscle screamed NO!

This wasn't the first time that my body betrayed me during a key moment. Despite my thorough mental preparation I often felt an uncomfortable knot in my stomach before big keynote presentations or important mental sessions with high profile teams. It was frustrating.

Why, when I am able to coach the mind to be geared towards top performance, can it all be so easily thwarted by the body?

In 2012 I experienced a series of high profile big tournament losses as part of my role as Mental Coach to various teams. It was the best and worst year of my life as a professional working in elite sport. I stood next to the Irish men's hockey team coach in Dublin at the end of the Olympic Qualifying Tournament Final when we lost 3-2 to Korea. The last goal was a cruel deflection with seconds left on the clock and victory would have meant qualification for the Olympic Games. (The last time an Irish team qualified was 1906.) In Townsville I shared the pain of the South African u19 cricket team after we lost to Australia in the semi-final of the u19 World Cup. At this point we've never been able to bring an u19 World Cup trophy home, in spite of very talented teams competing in the tournament. The 2012 team was one of our most talented yet. At the Olympic Games in London as part of the South African Men's hockey team we lost a series of close matches to finish 11 out of 12. This result meant we missed finishing in the crucial top six bracket which would have secured funding and the future of men's hockey in South Africa for the medium term.

All over the world I saw dreams of success in tatters.

The hurt of the various losses cut deeply. For many months I relived the trauma of the losses in my dreams and felt haunted by the images of disappointed, teary eyed players and coaches who had failed. It was traumatic for all involved and made me feel like a fraud as a professional. I wanted to hide from the world and the world of sports in particular. I thought about quitting sports work entirely in favour of 'safer' work which wouldn't leave me feeling like such a failure. At the same time, I could not shake the nagging question in the back of my mind: 'What am I missing?'

Over time I was able to debrief several of these athletes. I wanted to get really specific and review key moments by talking about what was happening on the outside (the game,) as well as what was happening for them on the inside (their self-talk, what they were focusing on and what they were feeling). By slowing the conversation down it was easier to pinpoint the true origin and cause of their mistakes. I started hearing things like:

'I had a stiff shoulder and then missed the key tackle on the goal scorer.' (Hockey)
'My hands were slow so I couldn't block the cross that lead to the goal.' (Hockey)
'My chest closed up as I ran in to bowl an important over and I couldn't land the ball where I wanted to. This was a key moment of the game I let slip.' (Cricket)
'My arms became tense as I played the shot that I got caught out on.' (Cricket)

In each case, skilful, hard-working athletes were let down by the tension in their bodies at key moments. In Dublin there was a stiff shoulder and slow hands. In Townsville it was tension in the arms and chest. In London it was sluggish feet and butterflies in the stomach not flying in formation. What was going on that even though the minds of these athletes were prepared for success their bodies worked against them during key moments?

In sport we often expect stiff arms, legs and bodies and so typically we don't think more deeply about physical tension from a mental point of view. However, what was different about this tension and stiffness is that it was temporary, as it disappeared outside of the pressure moment(s). It was a different kind of tension created in a different way.

Could it be that the unconscious fears linked to winning (or the prospect of losing) was being activated under extreme pressure and that these fears were linked to specific areas in the body?

Could an athlete's doubt about winning be linked to his or her sluggish feet? Could the fear that you are not good enough create tension in your hands? Could a lack of self-belief be trapped in your shoulders? Could the fear of letting others down create stiffness in your arms? Could you worrying about being embarrassed be responsible for your wobbly knees? Could the fear of choking cause chaos in your stomach?

Every athlete I debriefed shared that he was let down by tension in different parts of his body in key moments.

For nine more months I continued to obsessively review, question and research to find better answers to what was actually going on. This included attending diverse trainings and having endless discussions with my business partner Mike, my peers and experienced coaches. Finally, the pieces of the puzzle snapped together for my eureka moment.

Eight: **A solid foundation**
- the seven principles of Scanning

This chapter explains in detail the seven ideas, theories and principles which formed part of my research and played a key role in developing the *Scanning* technique. Whilst it's good to understand the background, it's not crucial for benefiting from the technique and you are welcome to skip ahead if this is not of interest to you.

1. The idea that tension in different parts of the body often hamper the performance of athletes during key moments came up when I did research for my previous book *Raising Talent in 2011/2012.* This led to me developing a technique I called the *Mind Body Integration* or MBI[17] technique (which won the Bronze award for contribution to Neuro-Semantics in 2012). It enabled me to coach some athletes some of the time about some of the blocks that was showing up in their body. Although this was a big breakthrough, it didn't work for enough people and didn't seem to 'find' all the blocks in the body. However, it was a great foundation to expand upon and *Scanning*, the core

---

[17] Dr L. Michael Hall's series of articles on Alfred Korzybski's work explain how we have three different layers of belief: the mental movies we make, the meanings we have about the movies and the meanings we hold in the body. It was this insight that led me to create the MBI technique.

technique of this book, is basically MBI Version 3.0.

2. In Neuro-Semantics the *Mind-to-Muscle* technique is a tool which aims to help us internalise ideas or beliefs to 'live in our body'. Put another way: to be in our core so we live with them being activated. These beliefs operate unconsciously and we don't need to consciously think about it in order to benefit. Even though I didn't experience a lot of success with the technique as a Meta-Coach, this idea has always fascinated me and I hoped to discover a way to implement it more effectively.

3. The numerous models of Neuro-Semantics and Meta-Coaching map out how not all beliefs are created equal and challenge coaches to find the key beliefs to facilitate positive change. To this end, Neuro-Semantics gave me the opportunity to see old and new things differently and this understanding allowed me to develop simple processes that were very powerful. (A robust coaching methodology is needed to coach the body and whilst my Meta-Coaching training provided a strong foundation for coaching the body, I believe the techniques and principles in this book provide new and important answers.)

4. The title of Candice Pert's audiobook, *Your body is your subconscious mind* had a huge impact on me (yes the title and not necessarily the audiobook itself). This lead me to asking what if that was true? What if the mind wasn't just located in

the brain[18], but in fact linked to the entire body?

5. I read Karl Dawson and Sasha Allenby's book *Matrix Reimprinting using EFT* and attended one of Karl's workshops which introduced me to Matrix Reimprinting[19]. It was one of the more powerful healing modalities that I have experienced. As part of the Matrix Reimprinting process there is a healing step of 'imagine telling every cell in your body that this is your new reality.' I wasn't always able to use my imagination to do that, but that thought stuck with me – what if I could get every cell in my body to hold a new empowering positive belief?

6. I read Alex Loyd's and Ben Johnson's book *The Healing Codes* and started experimenting by using the techniques for my own personal healing. It showed me that using your hands can be a beneficial tool in the mental healing and/or growth process. Over the next few years I discovered more research which has helped me understand the science behind using different hand shapes and positions to enhance healing and growth.

---

[18] Recent studies have shown that the brain, heart and gut all have their own 'mind' which together contribute to a person's wellbeing.

[19] Through Matrix Reimprinting I also got a chance to attend Sharon King's *Heal your birth, heal your life* workshop, which she has been running for many years before the release of her book of the same name in 2015.

Alex Loyd's more recent book *Beyond Willpower (2015)* introduced me to Dr Mitsuo Hiramatsu, a scientist at the Central Research Laboratory at Hamamatsu Photonics in Japan. Hiramatsu was able to prove that human hands[20] emit biophotons or Ultraweak Photon Emissions (UPEs) and that the shape of the hand creates different outputs of biophotons.

Another experiment by Dotta, Saroka and Persinger showed that these biophotons can be influenced by intention/thoughts. A third experiment by Bokkon, Salari, Tuszynski and Antal shows that biophotons can travel through our nervous system and can be captured and stored inside cells. This suggests that biophotons may provide a way to communicate information and transfer energy.

7. In 2010 when I was experimenting with sharks, dives, jumps and overall discomfort I developed a theory I called the *Body Energy Threshold Principle*. It explains how the body has an energy threshold which impacts how and when beliefs are stored and revealed. The principle came about as I wanted to understand why beliefs are sometimes locked in and exposed by a single moment, whilst at other times it takes several hours to hammer in a new belief or reveal an old one. It's also my experience that far too often, no amount of hammering (using

---

[20] Aside from the hands, Hiramatsu proved that the forehead and the soles of feet also emit biophotons.

a technique like affirmations) works. What I discovered is that the level of energy activated in the body determines whether and at what level a belief gets locked in or revealed.

Every individual has a unique energetic level and this is an important element which influences why belief change is easier for some than others. Unfortunately, traumatic experiences tend to carry much higher levels of energy and therefore the negative beliefs that may be created from these events are often easier stored. I discovered that during moments of intense energy, not only does the deep beliefs in the body get activated but it also presents a chance to influence and change the body's deep beliefs.

Based on these seven principles I created a technique called *Scanning* which first materialised as a method to release limiting beliefs in relation to winning in sport.

In 2008 I introduced a method I called 'creating movies' to help sports teams mentally prepare for game day. I tasked clients with creating vivid, high quality multi-sensory visualisations or 'movies' which they added positive meaning to. These movies showed them winning the game and created more confidence and more belief for many (but not all) athletes.

In 2013 I added *Scanning* as an extra step to the 'creating movies' process. The intention was to then *Scan* in the beliefs to support the win, or rather use the *Scanning* process to identify what beliefs were in the way of winning so that they could be removed. As my understanding deepened I encouraged my clients to create multiple game scenario movies: how they start, how they play their game, how they finish, how they play to their strengths, how they bounce back etc. These scenarios covered how they will effectively deal with the various difficult situations they could predict or foresee. I was very excited about the big difference that this approach made, but did not know at the time that there was still another more advanced level of *Scanning* to come.

The process of 'creating movies' and *Scanning* in supporting beliefs to enable a winning mindset revealed some challenges which needed to be addressed.

Over the next few years it became clear that a high quality winning movie, whilst very effective for some, did not always change a poor performance mindset. For instance, many athletes unknowingly reinforced their own negative beliefs when creating their movies. As an example an athlete who felt that he or she was not good enough could create a movie about winning, but unless the belief of not being good enough was specifically and accurately addressed in the movie it still remained.

So whilst *Scanning* was a major breakthrough in mental coaching in sports, it was not and is not a silver bullet. *Scanning* in movies still relies on the athlete being self-aware enough to identify all the relevant solutions they need, whilst creating their winning movie, in order to address their mental shortcomings. For *Scanning* in movies to be effective an athlete also needs strong mental skills, a deep mental understanding base and a healthy team environment/system. Over a few seasons of working with different sports teams, it became clear that a quality control checklist (which I describe in detail in this article[21]) is required for the process of *Scanning* in movies to be consistently successful.

At the time I concluded that a better way to benefit from *Scanning* without having to manage the risk meant focusing on *Scanning* specific beliefs rather than performance movies. The question of what specific positive beliefs will make the most positive difference lead me to develop the *Game Changer Protocol*. The question of how to work accurately to align deep beliefs with the mind and the body is answered in the next chapter.

---

[21] I eventually created a very structured and organised approach to match day preparation that solved many of these problems, for those that were willing to do the work. Read more about it at http://raisingtalentthebook.com/dynamic/

Nine: **A two-way conversation**
- Coaching the Body

In order to *Coach the Body*, it is important to understand that the unconscious mind can spontaneously speak through the body at any time about anything. As an example, having a 'gut feeling' is something most people not only experience, but are intuitively able to translate themselves. That 'gut feeling' is the unconscious mind wanting to be heard and speaking through the body.

Unfortunately, it is more common for the unconscious mind to speak through the body when we are experiencing pressure and it shows up in the form of a nervous stomach, racing heart, sweaty palms, dry mouth etc. This is the *Energy Threshold Principle* in action: when the body is experiencing intense energy, the unconscious mind is more likely to speak up and to give us messages in relation to that specific energy. The method of translating and working with these messages is called: *Coaching the Body*. Without it, nervous stomachs tend to stay nervous without understanding the exact cause, racing hearts keep racing and all other messages from the unconscious mind remain untranslated and unaddressed.

When we *Coach the Body* the first stage involves translating the body's messages. I refer to these messages, or energy which pops up in the body, as *Wobbles* (which need to be translated.) They act as a flashing light which indicates that the unconscious mind wants to speak. Some are easy to spot like 'gut feelings', a racing heart and sweaty palms. Others are subtler and need a technique like *Scanning* to be revealed. This brings us to:

Coaching the Body: Part A
How to translate the body's messages, a.k.a. *Wobbles*
The answer to how to translate specific body energy created by the unconscious mind (so that you can understand the message and use it for your benefit) is three fold.

1. **Ask 'What' questions instead of 'Why' questions**

   We often use the word or question 'Why' when trying to better understand things. The problem is that it's a logic based question and often implies that there is a single and/or simple reason for the problem. Situations and people can be complex and forcing a simple answer from a complex situation doesn't work. 'Why did you do that?', 'Why are you getting defensive?', 'Why did you make that mistake?' Posing the question 'Why' often fails to discover the true answer. This is because most 'Why' questions scan the conscious mind for an answer and when it can't find one it starts to install an answer in the unconscious mind. This leaves the questioner uncertain of the correct answer and often defensive. Most 'Why' questions install rather than discover.

   'What' questions are different. 'What's that about?', 'What's stopping you?', 'What is this emotion about?' 'What's holding this in place?' 'What' questions jump into the movie playing in the mind in relation to the question and starts to process the information related to it. By asking a series of 'What' questions eventually (and this might take some time), an answer will emerge. It often starts out sounding vague and unformed, e.g. 'I'm angry', 'I feel uncomfortable', 'I have doubts', 'I have this voice in my head saying this is wrong.'

At that point it's important to get true clarity to the question by using more questions to get to the specifics. 'What are you angry about?', 'What are you uncomfortable about?', 'What doubts are you having … About what?' 'Whose voice is saying this is wrong?', 'Wrong in what way?'

You may need to use several rounds of 'What' questions if your original answers don't provide enough clarity and to get to the heart of what's going on. 'I'm angry about my father.' - 'What are you angry about your father about?' 'I have this doubt that I am not enough' – 'Not enough what?' 'It's my mom's voice telling me this is wrong.' – 'Wrong in that I should never be thinking this?'

2. **Point 'What' questions at specific energy or (if not possible) at a specific thought.**
When working with *Wobbles* (messages from the unconscious mind that show up as specific energy in the body) you should focus on one thing at a time and stay with that one thing until

the answer emerges. Emotions are a great example of specific energy. 'What's going on that my jaw is clenched in anger?', 'What's this fear about?', 'What are these nerves about?'

It's important to remember that the unconscious mind can speak up via any part of the body, especially during the *Scanning* process. As the whole of the body is the unconscious mind any part of the mind/body can hold limiting beliefs or blocked energy.

During *Scanning* my clients have reported feeling an energy *Wobble* in the throat, neck, shoulder, chest, lower back, stomach, hand, thigh, knee, calf, below the eyes, below the ear etc. A client in Malaysia even shared feeling energy in her big toe!

Sometimes the link is a clear metaphor or idiom: 'I feel pressure on my shoulders' (heavy load), 'I feel pain in my back after being betrayed' (stabbed in the back). Other times the link is due to an injury or accident which has emotional baggage lingering in the body, for example when a knee acts up long after the physical injury has healed. Sometimes there is no apparent logic to why someone's left hip is activated in a *Scan*, other than the answer they receive when they ask the 'What's that about?' question. (By the way, the Malaysian client with the energy in her big toe found that her answer was frustration with herself as she felt she was always tripping herself up in life.)

The question 'What's that about?' can also be used to discover which belief or beliefs are responsible for negative thoughts that have plagued someone over time. However, this can be more challenging as you have to trace the answer and the structure of what's going on from and through the conscious mind. Many more layered 'What's that about?' questions will need to be asked in order to find the structure that's sitting in the unconscious mind, (by tracing it from the conscious mind). It's very do-able, it's just harder to do than following energy. I recommend always focusing on body energy first as it's easier to work with and you jump straight into the unconscious mind which takes you a lot closer to the core of what's going on.

3. **Be patient and open about the answer**

When you are *Coaching the Body*, the conscious mind and the unconscious mind are having an intense conversation, whilst the body is acting as the translator between the two minds. This takes time and the answer often starts out as being vague. Answers can be silly, embarrassing and harsh. They might even feel childish, but they remain real for the individual and therefore need to be treated with non-judgement and the necessary curiosity, until they can be dealt with appropriately.

When asking the 'What's that about?' question you need to give yourself at least 30-60 seconds to consider it. If you can, look at the part of the body where the energy is coming from. If you struggle to get an answer it can help to bow your head for added focus. Some questions may take minutes to be answered, others may need more time. That's okay. Just keep checking in with the same 'What's that about?' question. When you combine these three steps when working with the body it is called translating a *Wobble*.

Once we've translated the body's messages or *Wobbles*, the second stage of *Coaching the Body* is to resolve the *Wobbles* which showed up during the translation process.

***Coaching the Body*: Part B**
How to work with your answer using *The Decision Tree*
In order to resolve the *Wobbles* you need to decide which action to take for each one and to do so you can make use of *The Decision Tree*. It offers three simple choices: Keep, Solve or Let Go. The choice needs to be made intuitively and it's okay if you choose the 'wrong' action at first as you can simply choose again until your body tells you that you have made the right choice for that specific *Wobble*. As soon as the 'right' decision is made the *Wobbles'* energy will either disappear or shift.

The Decision Tree

1. **Keep**

    If what you have found is 100% positive for you, then it's important to acknowledge and reinforce it. This is often the case for 'butterflies in the stomach' where it is actually positive stress or eustress which is getting you ready to be your best. The only thing that doesn't fit is that at some level you have mislabelled this positive energy as negative. Now is your chance to label it correctly. You do this by first checking in: 'Is this 100% positive for me?' Once you have an internal 'Yes' to that question focus on that energy and thank it, 'Thank you for helping me be my best.' If the energy is accurately dealt with it will dissolve. If the energy moves or changes it means that a new message is emerging and you need to translate that new message and use it is an input into *The Decision Tree*.

2. **Solve**

    To find a solution any one of the following three options can be applied:

    - Action(s) need to be taken
    - Conversations need to be started
    - Hidden benefits need to be uncovered

    2.1 **Action(s) need to be taken**

    Ask yourself: 'What needs to be done to solve this?' As you reflect and come up with a solution make sure it is specific and measurable and attached to a specific day or time. For example, a starting solution of, 'I need to build my relationship with my mother in-law (who interferes with my parenting)' could become, 'After Sunday night dinner at the in-laws I will ask my mother-in-law to join me in the study for an important conversation. Then I will share that I care for her deeply and want our relationship to grow and to do so I would like to discuss our different parenting styles.'

To test the solution focus on where you experienced the *Wobble* and tell it the solution you have come up with. If what you have worked out is an accurate solution the energy will disappear, change or move. If the energy moves or changes, you need to translate this new *Wobble*. Whilst focusing on the new energy ask yourself, 'What's that about?' to discover the next layer of what you need to work with. Then use *The Decision Tree* to work with the new message. If the energy disappears completely you have your solution. Write it down, commit to taking that action and then continue with your *Scan* (if you were *Scanning*).

2.2 Conversations need to be started

What needs to be said that hasn't been said yet? To who? In what way? Perhaps you need to have a courageous conversation? Maybe you need to apologise or make a difficult yet important request? Could it be about asking for forgiveness or forgiving yourself?

To test the solution focus on where you experienced the *Wobble* and tell it the solution you have come up with. If what you have worked out is an accurate solution the energy will disappear, change or move. If the energy moves or changes, you need to translate this new *Wobble*. Whilst focusing on the new energy ask yourself, 'What's that about?' to discover the next layer of what you need to work with. Then use *The Decision Tree* to work with the new message. If the energy disappears completely you have your solution. Write it down, commit to taking that action and then continue with your *Scan* (if you were *Scanning*).

2.3 Hidden benefits need to be uncovered

It may be that you are unable to let go of something that clearly affects you negatively. For example procrastination, self-judgement or a bad memory. When this happens it often means that you are receiving a higher level benefit by holding on to that style. This benefit is often unconscious. Procrastination might provide you with more safety, self-judgement might provide you with more restraint, holding on to a bad memory might be a powerful reminder to avoid any similar situations. The first step is to ask yourself, 'What benefit am I getting from X?' (where X is your procrastination, self-judgement or a bad memory). This answer may take a while to form and that's okay. There may be more than one benefit. Once you have your answer or answers you need to use them in an updated Permission Release statement (see 3. Let Go). 'I give myself full permission to let go of my X whilst keeping my Y' or in this case, 'I give myself full permission to let go of my procrastination whilst keeping my sense of having more safety.' Or in another example, 'I give myself full permission to let go of the pain and negatives of my bad memory whilst keeping the healthy lessons.'

If the energy moves or changes, you need to translate this new *Wobble*. Whilst focusing on the new energy ask yourself, 'What's that about?' to discover the next layer of what you need to work with. Then use *The Decision Tree* to work with the new message. If the energy disappears completely you have your solution and then continue with your *Scan* (if you were *Scanning*).

3. **Let Go**

When you translate a *Wobble* and the answer is non-supportive, doesn't make you happy, or doesn't help you to achieve your goals it's time to let go. Maybe you have an old belief that is now out of date? Maybe that belief is child-like thinking which needs to be let go of? Maybe it is created from fear and doesn't offer any value?

Typically, you would work with a professional coach to track and release all the layers of limiting thinking and to process the different types of conversations that can emerge from *Scanning*. Instead of adding chapters to the book and layers of complexity I have simplified the release process to be as easy to use as possible, yet still effective.

My preferred method for letting go of limiting beliefs is to use what I call a Permission Release statement.

3.1 Permission Release

In order to let go of a limiting belief you must focus on the words that make up the belief and say to yourself 'I give myself full permission to let go of as much of this as I can for today.' If you are ready, then it will be a full release and all the energy will disappear. It will feel like exhaling or energy shifting in the body. You will feel a little lighter.

It could also be the case, for whatever reason, that you cannot fully release the limiting belief. However, often letting go of a small part of a big thing is just what's needed. If you keep chipping away at it over time, it will soon be dealt with fully.

3.2 Permission Release Advanced

If you want to and are ready to do some slightly more advanced work and there is still some energy left after the statement 'I give myself full permission to let go of as much of this as I can for today' then focus on the energy that remains.

If the energy didn't move ask yourself, 'What is stopping me from letting this go?' Then wait for your answer. When you get an answer use it as an input into *The Decision Tree*.

If the energy moves or changes, you need to translate this new *Wobble*. Whilst focusing on the new energy ask yourself, 'What's that about?' to discover the next layer of what you need to work with. Then use *The Decision Tree* to work with the new message. If the energy disappears completely you have your solution and then continue with your *Scan* (if you were *Scanning*).

Exercise to practice:
1. Think of a recent experience when you received body feedback/a *Wobble*. (Nervous stomach, racing heart, pressure on shoulders, heavy feeling in the gut, etc.)
2. Try to remember as much about that moment as possible so that you can experience it all again clearly: what you saw, heard and felt. By slowing down the movie in your mind you should start to feel some of the body feedback/*Wobble* again. If you can recreate some of the feeling(s) again you can translate and work with it.

3. Translate that *Wobble* with the 'What's that about?' question.
4. Use *The Decision Tree* to coach yourself to a more resourceful outcome.

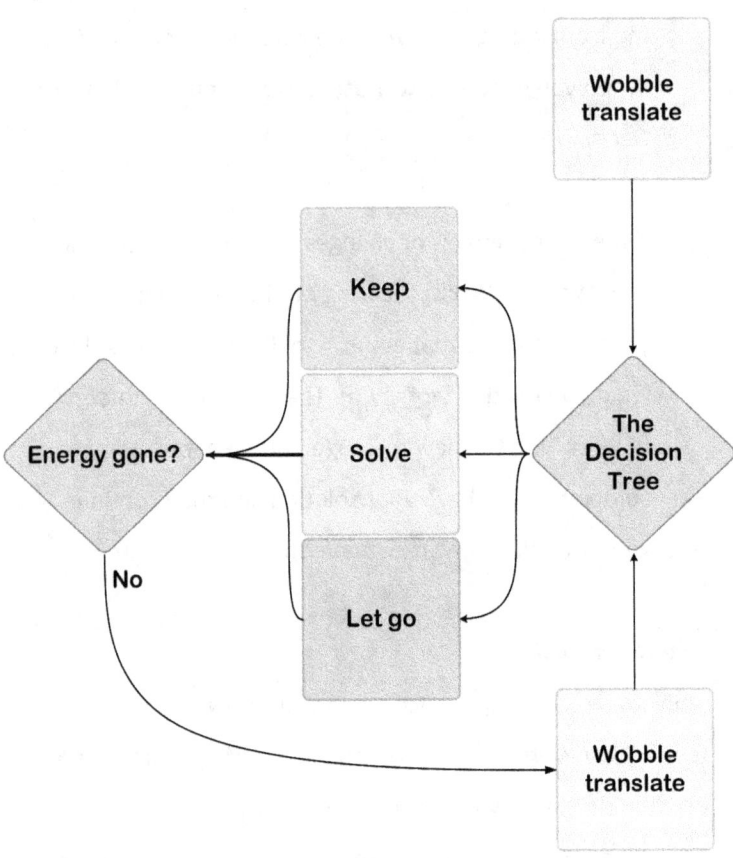

Key Principles of *Coaching the Body*:

1. Core beliefs live within the body. Different beliefs live in different parts of the body (neck, shoulder, chest, stomach, jaw, throat, knee etc.)
2. The body has an energy threshold, which means that for new beliefs to get into the body or to trigger old beliefs locked in the body, they need to have a certain level of energy attached to them. This level is different for different people.
3. Specific energy activated in the body is a message from your unconscious mind that needs to be translated with the 'What's that about?' question.
4. Specific energy that has been translated with the 'What's that about?' question can be accurately and effectively addressed by using *The Decision Tree* of Keep/Solve/Let go. You will know that the message linked to the energy has been partially addressed if the energy moves or that it has been fully addressed if the energy is released or dissolved.
5. Each time the energy moves or changes in the body it reveals a new message that needs to be translated with the 'What's that about?' question.

Ten: **Aligning mind and body**
- introducing Scanning

Now that we know how to accurately *Coach the Body* and deal effectively with energy *Wobbles* and their related messages using *The Decision Tree*, it's time to pull all the pieces together.

The first stage of *Scanning* involves choosing one of the 10 healthy self-esteem beliefs that make up the *Game Changer Protocol* (Chapter Six). In order to prevent unhealthy beliefs and excuses from limiting the impact of *Scanning*, each healthy belief has been matched with a set-up question. For example: the first healthy belief of the *Game Changer Protocol* is 'I am okay'.

The challenge with a broad proclamation like 'I am okay' is that it can mean many different things to many different people and if you are struggling you might find a way to justify that you are okay, even if you aren't. Therefore, in order to avoid that we need a strong set-up question to accompany 'I am okay.' For example:

Healthy belief: 'I'm okay'
I'm okay set-up: 'What will it mean to me if I could know and experience that I'm okay, fully and completely, no matter what?'

You will find all ten of the *Game Changer Protocol* beliefs and their matching set-up questions in Chapter Thirteen.

The second stage of *Scanning* involves creating positive healthy energy to get the body to speak up about something specific. This process is called *Supercharging*.

The only way I previously knew how to get my body to speak up was to put myself in harm's way. You might have experienced your body 'speaking up' during high pressure or stressful moments as well? However, I am not asking you to swim with sharks or jump off tall buildings in order to work reactively with what your body tells you. There is another way to get your body to speak up not just in general, but about a very specific healthy belief.

To get your body to speak up we *Supercharge* by asking a series of 'What would it mean to me?' questions about the answer you get from the set-up question. For example:

I'm okay set-up: 'What will it mean to me if I could know and experience that I'm okay, fully and completely, no matter what?'

Possible answer: 'I will enjoy my life again.'
This answer (and the ones to follow) need to continue to be *Supercharged* with the 'What would that mean to me?' question. (Each answer refers to the previous question).
Question: 'What would that (I will enjoy my life again) mean to me?'
Possible answer: 'I will be more myself.'
Question: 'What would that (I will be more myself) mean to me?'

Possible answer: 'I will stay true to myself.'

Question: 'What would that (I will stay true to myself) mean to me?'

Possible answer: 'I can go after my dreams.'

Question: 'What would that (I can go after my dreams) mean to me?'

Possible answer: 'My life will be awesome!'

NB: Make sure that all your answers (including the answer to your set-up question) are positively stated (what I want) before you answer the next, 'What would that mean to me?' question. To convert any negatively stated answers (e.g. 'I won't be scared anymore', 'I won't hold myself back,' 'I won't be unhappy.') into something positive you ask yourself, 'So if I don't have that (negative answer) what (positive) will I have instead?'

As you add more meaning the answers will most likely get deeper for you and you will feel more energy. If you answer six or seven 'What would that mean to me?' questions, it's very likely that the positive energy will start to show up on your face – in the form of a smile or twinkling eyes.

If there is enough energy to show up on the face, there is enough energy to get into the body.

Once the energy shows up on your face (with a smile or twinkling eyes), it's time for stage three, the *Open Palm Scan*.

It can be difficult to have the concentration, imagination or precision to just visualise the positive energy from the *Supercharging* step working through the body. However, it doesn't need to be that hard and it becomes much easier if you are able to do this slowly and deliberately.

The *Open Palm Scan* is based on the principles behind progressive relaxation and the CAT scan. When I refer to progressive relaxation I mean slowing down to focus on specific parts of the body so that your whole body is impacted. When you tell your whole body to relax at once it isn't nearly as effective as focusing on each individual muscle in the body, relaxing one at a time and working your way from your toes to your head or vice versa. Slowing down and focusing on specific parts of the body is also fundamental to how a CAT scan works.

For those who are not familiar with the CAT scanner device – it's a medical tool known to those in the field as a computerised tomography (CT) scan. It looks to me like a big beige 2-metre-tall vertical doughnut attached to the top of a medical bed. The bed sits inside the inner circle of the doughnut. The doughnut glides from the top of the bed to the bottom like a magician using a hoop to show how an assistant is sleeping in mid-air. As it glides it takes a series of X-ray images and a computer processes those images to tell a story. As you lie down on the bed the doughnut shape scans slowly from your head to your toes (or focuses on a specific part of the body). The purpose of the CAT scan is to make invisible injuries visible.

Now - think of your hand as a handheld CAT scanner which allows you to discover where the invisible internal 'injuries' are, or to be more accurate in this case, where the contradictory beliefs locked in the body are.

Raise your dominant hand to be level with your eyes, palm open with fingers pointing left or right (depending on which is your dominant hand) and elbow up. (The shape of your hand is important,[22] as it magnifies the effect.) Imagine all the positive answers you unpacked from your 'What would that mean to me?' questions getting brighter and stronger and beginning to travel out of your open palm hand like a gentle, yet powerful thruster. It may have a colour, texture or sound, it may not – whatever feels right for you. Point that thruster at yourself and slowly begin to move it down your body. As you point your thruster at yourself give yourself the instruction, 'I give myself full permission for every cell in my body to have X,' where X is all the positive *Supercharged* meanings and energy that you have created.

---

[22] Mitsuo Hiramatsu, a research scientist, has proven that different hand positions create different amounts of energy. My use of the open palm hand shape is based on his research.

Aligning mind and body - *introducing Scanning*

Start at the very top of your head and slowly *Scan* down to your feet. It should take about 20-30 seconds to *Scan* from top to bottom, if there are no *Wobbles* to work with. You should feel some level of energy transfer in your body where your open palm is facing – if you don't, *Supercharge* some more by answering more,' What would that mean to me?' questions.

If and when you hit a *Wobble,* it means that your unconscious mind is speaking up through your body. Focus on the part of your body that is giving you feedback; a knotted stomach, tingling in the hands, heaviness on the shoulder or just a slight 'bump' or '*Wobble*' you have found. As you focus on that area (look at it if you can) ask yourself the question, 'What is this about?' This is called translating a *Wobble*. Make sure that you are looking down at your body as you ask this question, as it will help you to connect more with the body. Wait patiently for any feedback from your body. Your question is a body question and the answer will often emerge slowly. Sit for 20 to 30 seconds (if need be) with the question and see what comes to mind. If this is your first *Scan*, you might have to wait even longer, just keep asking yourself slowly the same question, 'What is that about?' and explore the first thought/memory/idea/metaphor that pops into your head. You may need to ask more 'What' questions for clarity – as described in Chapter Nine.

Once you have the message that has been translated from your unconscious mind through your body it's time to move on to stage four of the *Scanning* process, *The Decision Tree*. (At this point you can drop your hand to save you from potential arm fatigue.)

I describe how to use *The Decision Tree* in-depth in Chapter Nine, however, for the sake of clarity here is a high level summary of how it works.

After a *Wobble* has been translated using the 'What is this about?' question there are three high level options for addressing it via *The Decision Tree*: Keep, Solve or Let go. Use your intuition to explore which option is best for you and you know you are making progress when the energy of the *Wobble* moves, changes or disappears. If the energy moves or changes it means there is another layer of message that needs to be translated again and another round of using *The Decision Tree* is needed. If the energy disappears you have accurately dealt with the *Wobble* and now you need to connect with your *Supercharging* energy again and continue your *Open Palm Scan*.

If you have completed your *Open Palm Scan* in that you have *Scanned* yourself from head to toe and back again and dealt with all your *Wobbles*, your whole body should be brimming with positive energy. Now it is time for stage five, Lock it down.

You Lock it down by asking yourself 'What does it mean to me that my mind and body is more and more aligned?' And then ask

Aligning mind and body - *introducing Scanning*

yourself 'What does this mean to me?' five times or more as a response to the answers you receive.

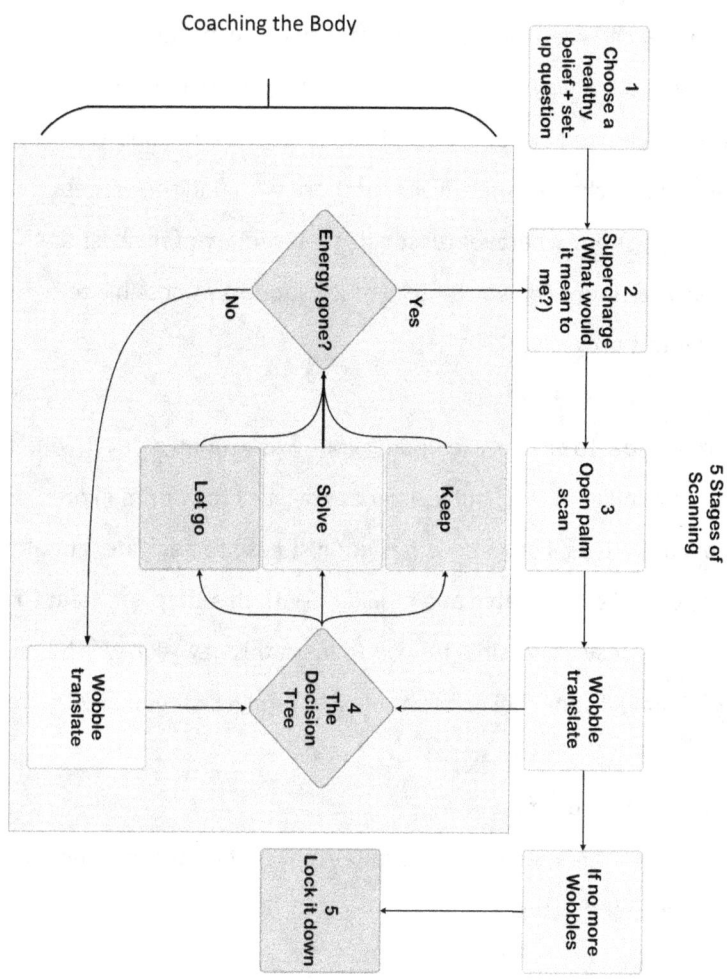

Eleven: Uncluttering the mind
- preparing for Scanning

When I teach *Scanning* in a workshop environment the initial responses are always very varied. These responses range from curious, keen and excited to sceptical, confused and doubtful. I've included this chapter specifically for those who find the process challenging – for whatever reason. It's a summary of my best tips and advice to provide you with as much support as possible to master this powerful skill.

Learning how to *Scan* is like finding your way around a new town. It feels unfamiliar at first, but as long as you stick to your map or follow directions it soon becomes not just easy to navigate, but also starts to feel comfortable and familiar. With this chapter I want to make it as easy as possible for you to learn this new skill which I'm confident will soon feel comfortable and familiar for you.

Preparing for your first *Scan*

Preparation is made up of three important parts: Attitude, Self-awareness and Setup.

1. **Attitude – getting rid of negative thinking styles**

    Scanning is a new skill based on some new ideas. If you fill your mind with curiosity, openness and patience you are likely to not just learn this skill, but to learn it quickly. A thinking style which leans predominantly towards criticism, cynicism and scepticism will interfere with the value you can get from *Scanning* and I urge you to please let go of this type of thinking. If you can't let it go I challenge you to set aside as much of your doubt, cynicism and scepticism as possible for just 20 minutes.

For *Scanning* to be effective you need to:

- Believe it can be effective or at the very least be open to that idea.
- Be playful, or at least commit to being more playful.
- Acknowledge and be proud of the progress that you are making instead of focusing on how far you still have to go. It will help you to be more positive and even excited about moving small steps forward.
- Remove questions like 'Will this work for me?' If you have to ask yourself a question, rather ask the more effective 'How much will this work for me?' question.
- Be open to the possibility that this could all be easier than you think.

As you work through this process new negative beliefs you never even considered before will emerge and this is a really positive indicator. It means that as the negative beliefs you've held on to are replaced with healthy beliefs, other beliefs you didn't even realise were holding you back are becoming accessible so that you can deal with them as well.

2. **Self-awareness – understanding your beliefs**

    It's important to check that you have a healthy reference for all the key words in the various *Scans*. Words like belonging, acceptance and worthy for example can hold various meanings for different people. For instance, 'I belong' as an idea might be a huge challenge to you, as you don't have a current reference of what true belonging is like. If that is the case, try to recall a time or moment in your life when you did feel a sense of belonging, even if it was for just a moment. What was that like? Can you choose to focus on that feeling of belonging without any rules or conditions, when you do the 'I belong' *Scan*? It may be that even your memories have negative conditions or emotions linked to them and you need to spend some time imagining what it might be like to truly belong, or to truly accept yourself.

    When I started working to improve my own self-worth I discovered that my version of words such as acceptance and worthiness were distorted. I had to reference the only relationship in my life where I felt 100% unconditional acceptance and that was with my cat Buffy. If you don't have any personal positive references for words like worthy, acceptance, belonging etc. you should imagine what it might be like to have that using a friend's example, a favourite book character or something that resonates that you saw in a movie or on TV. If you use your imagination or borrow from someone on TV or from a book, make sure that there are no negatives or downsides to that example.

3. **Setup – getting the time and place right**

    Find a quiet place to do your *Scanning* work where you know you won't be disturbed for about 20 minutes. (You probably won't need all that time, but just set it aside anyway.) Turn off your phone and remove all other possible interruptions. If you're struggling to focus because your head is too busy, rather choose another time or clear your head by writing down a to do list which can be set aside for 20 minutes.

    Try to relax. If you feel most relaxed in the evening after a hot bath, shower or in the morning after an invigorating jog try to schedule your *Scanning* session around the same time. You can also listen to relaxing music. If those methods don't work for you, I recommend Heart Breathing. This is an effective relaxation technique which allows you to 'get into your body'. Heart Breathing is described in **APPENDIX B** at the back of the book.

Twelve: **Step by step**
- your very first Scan

Before we get down to it I just want to reiterate that getting feedback from your body is a slow process requiring patience. Once you ask a specific 'What's that about?' question you need to wait ... and as you keep that question in mind ... wait some more. For first time *Scanners* it can take up to a minute or more of sitting with a question to get feedback. And that's okay.

Scanning step by step:

1. Get a pen and a blank piece of paper. Draw a line in the middle of the page and split it into two columns: A and B. Once you are sitting down comfortably, feeling relaxed and with all possible disturbances removed write down in Column A at the bottom of the page: 'I am okay.' You should start at the bottom of the page and work your way up. (The belief 'I am okay' is the first healthy belief you are going to *Scan* in.)

2. The next step is to write down the answer to the 'I am okay' set-up question, 'What would it mean to me if I could know and experience that I am okay fully and completely no matter what?' If your answer is positively stated write it down, one line up, in Column A. If your answer is about what you don't want, for example, 'I won't be scared anymore' write it down in Column B (one line up) and ask yourself the question: 'So if I am not *that* what would I be instead?' Write that answer in

Column A on the same line.

3. Now think about your last answer in Column A and ask yourself: 'Having that, what would that mean to me?' and write the answer down one line up. If it's positively stated it falls into Column A and negatively falls into Column B.

4. Keep on answering the 'Having that what would that mean to me?' question five times or more whilst focusing on the last answer in Column A. You must still use the same writing process (Column A for positively stated and Column B for negatively stated). The process of building up this positive energy is called *Supercharging*. Stop doing this step only when you start to feel yourself smile or your face feels full of positive energy.

5. Focus on taking all the positive energy from the words written down in Column A and imagine *Scanning* it into every cell of your body. Do it slowly from your head down to your feet and back again as if you were using a handheld CAT scanner – your hand being the scanner. (It's important to actually use your hand.)

6. Form an open palm gesture with your hand - (an open hand shape with the palm facing inwards, towards yourself and your elbow up in line with your ears). Now tell every cell in your body: 'I give myself full permission to have *this*' where *this* is all

the positive *Supercharged* meanings and energy you have created in Column A. Slowly move your hand (*Open Palm Scan*) from the top of your head, down to your face, neck, torso, stomach, lower body and legs - all the way down to your feet, so that every cell in every part of your body can now have *this*. Then move slowly up again. It should take about 20 to 30 seconds to move all the way down and another 20 to 30 seconds for moving all the way up, if you have no *Wobbles* or 'interruptions.'

7. If you feel a *Wobble* or 'interruption', write down (on a new page) where in the body you are experiencing the *Wobble* (e.g. neck, chest, stomach etc.) Now focus on the *Wobble* and ask yourself the question: 'What's this about?' (This process is called translating a *Wobble*.) This answer will emerge slowly, so focus on the energy of the *Wobble* and keep the 'What's that about?' question in mind for 60-90 seconds – an answer will begin to form which will probably start out as being vague. Don't judge it, just explore it. Once you have your first answer write it down next to where you wrote what the source of the *Wobble* is.

8. Once you have your first answer you may need to ask more 'What's that about?' or other clarity questions: 'Whose voice is that?', 'Who says that it's impossible?', 'How do you know this will never work for you?', 'Doubts about what?'... etc. Keep asking clarifying questions until you can create a specific movie

in your mind about what the *Wobble* is about.

9. Once the message is clear use *The Decision Tree* to Keep, Solve or Let go this message.

10. If the answer is Keep: thank that part of you for helping you be your best and the energy of the *Wobble* should disappear. If the answer is Solve: work out the best way to solve this (action, conversation or hidden benefits need to be uncovered). If you have solved it accurately the energy should disappear. If you have partially solved it, the energy will change or move. If that happens write down where the new energy is or the new level of energy (if it hasn't moved) and use the 'What's that about?' question to translate this new *Wobble*. Write it down and then use *The Decision Tree* to work with the next layer of what's going on. If you want to Let go: Focus on the phrase you want to let go and say to yourself 'I give myself full permission to let go of as much of this as I can for today.' If you have partially let it go, the energy will change or move. If that happens write down where the new energy is or the new level of energy (if it hasn't moved) and use the 'What's that about?' question to translate this new *Wobble*. Write it down and use *The Decision Tree* to work with the next layer of what is going on.

11. You will know when you've effectively dealt with a *Wobble* as the energy will no longer be there. Once that happens, it's time to reconnect with the built-up energy of the *Supercharge* by

either reading through the words you have written down in Column A from the bottom of the page up, or by answering the meaning questions again. Once you feel the energy on your face again use the *Open Palm Scan* moving down from the position of your last *Wobble*. *Scan* all the way to your feet and back again, (going up and down should take you around 40 seconds if there are no *Wobbles*).

12. Once you have addressed all your *Wobbles* and have either dealt with them fully or made progress with them (as is the case when you are chipping away at letting something go), it's time to Lock it down. You lock it down by asking yourself, 'What does it mean to me that I am more and more aligned with being okay?' (or whichever new empowering belief that you are focusing on). Then once you have that answer ask yourself 'What does that mean to me?' five times or more. You need to follow the same rules as before, if it is negatively stated write it in Column B and then find the positively stated answer instead, 'So If I don't have that, what will I have instead?'

This step-by-step process can be used to *Scan* in any of the 10 *Game Changer Protocol* beliefs.

Thirteen: **10 weeks for 10 beliefs**
- your self-esteem journey

Before we go further, I need to point out that it's important that you've read and followed the instructions in Chapter Twelve. Remember, this is a practitioner book and therefore it's not enough to just read the theory, you must also apply the *Scanning* technique for it to make a real difference in your life.

Once you fully understand and have experienced your first 'I am okay' *Scan*, it's important to keep up the momentum by committing to 10 weeks of *Scanning* in the 10 beliefs of the *Game Changer Protocol*.

You might recall from Chapter Three that we've identified three categories of self-esteem: healthy, conditional and low. Regardless of what level you find yourself at you will be able to achieve healthy self-esteem by committing to 10 weeks of the *Game Changer Protocol*. If you are already living with healthy self-esteem the programme will reinforce this and empower you further.
It's important that you follow each and every step in the order I have arranged them, no matter where you find yourself on the self-esteem scale. If you have any particular positive belief fully in place

when you *Scan* that same belief the effect[23] will be energising and uplifting, which further reinforces that positive belief. I have structured the 10 beliefs into a one per week schedule and I recommend focusing on one per week to start off with. However, if you have enough energy left after a session you can add another one or two beliefs per *Scanning* session.

If you still find objections during *Scanning* at the end of a week, keep working with that belief for four or more days in a row until everything is clear and no further objections pop up.

For each belief I have specified the set-up question that you will be *Supercharging*. Once you have your set-up question, follow the instructions in Chapter Twelve word for word, replacing the healthy belief in Step 1 and the set-up question in Step 2.

To get maximum benefit you need to *Scan* in all 10 beliefs.

Week 1
I'm okay set-up: What would it mean to me if I could know and experience that I am 100% okay, fully and completely, no matter what?

---

[23] A client remarked that to him *Scanning* is like taking five Berocca's (An energising effervescent drink containing vitamin B and vitamin C which is very popular in South Africa)

Week 2

I take full responsibility set-up: What would it meant to me if I could fully acknowledge, own and have choice over all my beliefs, thoughts, emotions, words and behaviours (even the parts I don't like about myself) – including my internal voice and what would that mean if I could take full responsibility for what is mine and let go of what is not, no matter what?

Week 3

I matter set-up: What would it mean to me if I could fully know and experience that I matter, no matter what?

Week 4

I belong set-up: What would it mean to me if I could know and experience that I belong, fully and completely in all the ways that count for me[24], no matter what?

Week 5

I am enough set-up: What would it mean to me if I could know and experience that I am enough, fully and completely, no matter what?

---

[24] 'In all the ways that count for me' is an important addition to that set-up question as there are some groups that we probably wouldn't want to belong to, like the lazy group or the miserable group.

Week 6

I have what it takes set-up: What would it mean to me if I could know and experience that I have what it takes fully and completely no matter what?

Week 7

I fully accept all of myself set-up: What would it mean to me if I could know and experience that I accept all of myself, fully and completely, no matter what?

Week 8

I am good enough set-up: What would it mean to me if I could know and experience that I am good enough, fully and completely, no matter what?

Week 9

I am a work in progress (Growth mindset) set-up: What would it mean to me if I believed, fully and completely, that all my abilities, even my most basic ones, could be developed and improved upon even if it takes some time no matter what?

Week 10

I am worthy of connection, love and belonging set-up: What would it mean to me if I could know and experience that I am worthy of connection, love and belonging, fully and completely, no matter what?

Maintenance

It is both liberating and invigorating to be free from limiting beliefs and to live a life of healthy self-esteem. You will be so much better equipped to deal with life's curveballs, but it doesn't mean there will be no more curveballs coming and significant emotional events can have an impact on your healthy self-esteem beliefs. I recommend a maintenance plan of checking in every three to six months.

Just *Scan* in three to four beliefs per day for three days and if you need to spend more time on a *Scan* keep doing it daily until your first thought at the beginning of a *Scan* is 'I've got this' or 'of course that is true' – or anything along those lines. If you have the time and mental energy, you can even do all 10 *Scans* in one day – it's up to you.

Fourteen: **Staying connected**
- a call for community

I firmly believe that by freeing yourself from limiting beliefs and developing healthy self-esteem you will be able to not only change your life, but also help improve the lives of those who know you, work with you and love you.

I've been able to improve my own life in immeasurable ways through the development of my self-esteem. However, I don't dare take it for granted and therefore I don't hesitate to turn to the tools available when my fears and ego trip me up and threaten my healthy beliefs.

Scanning is a brand new technique and the community it has been introduced to is still relatively small. Through the publication of this book and the success stories shared by those who've completed the programme I believe that the technique and specifically the *Game Changer Protocol* will become much more mainstream as it has the power to help millions of people become the best versions of themselves.

It has been extremely rewarding to witness the transformation in clients who've completed the programme and I would like nothing more than for the *Game Changer Protocol* to help each and every person struggling with limiting beliefs and low self-esteem. I also encourage therapists and coaches to use these techniques and

Staying connected - *a call for community*

processes in their private practices and I've made *Game Changer Protocol* technical training available to professionals in the field. I trust that a practitioner community will soon emerge.

To stay connected and up to date with news and happenings, you can visit the website www.gamechangerprotocol.com

I am excited about the healing and growth which is about to follow, as well the rich learnings we will be able to share and discuss as a community.

Tim Goodenough

Fifteen: **Troubleshooting**
- some additional support

Over several years of teaching *Scanning* in workshops and in my private practice I have experienced some unique responses and questions. I have collated many of these questions and answers in this chapter to serve as extra support to you.

1. ***Scanning* makes me feel negative**

    When negative feelings emerge during *Scanning* the three most likely culprits are:

    1.1 Asking the 'What would that mean to me?' question can result in a negative answer. If you do not convert this into a positive answer it means you carry on asking the 'What would that mean to me?' question about what you *don't* want. This can create negative energy and keep you from moving forward. To solve this, you need to convert what you don't want to what you *do* want, each and every time you find an answer that is expressed in the negative. For example, if the answer is: 'I won't be afraid anymore' you need to convert it to something which is stated positively, for example: 'What will I be instead (if I am not afraid anymore)? Possible answer: 'I will be courageous and real.' Then continue with the *Supercharging* questions: 'What would that mean to me?' (that I am courageous and real).

1.2 Feeling tired and drained after *Scanning* may be interpreted by some people as a negative experience. However, it's important to consider that major shifts in thinking can drain a lot of energy. I recommend a nap if possible, otherwise make sure you get a good night's sleep and drink plenty of water. Remember the reason you are feeling this way is because of all the positive changes happening in your mind and body. Change is happening!

1.3 If the series of 'What would that mean to me?' questions create negative answers for you, which you are truly unable to convert into a positive answer, you can change the set-up question to: 'What would it mean to me if I could feel more and more safe and more and more okay than I feel right now?' However, if you are in this mental space where you can't find any positive answers I highly recommend working with a specialist coach or therapist to support you getting back to your best self.

2. **What do I do if *Supercharging* my set-up statement causes me to burst into tears?**
If you burst into tears it is often a sign that this particular *Scan* is very relevant to you right now. It's important to welcome the emotion and to not try to fight it off or distance yourself from it. Dealing with and being okay with this emotion will

help you to move through it and receive the benefit of processing this emotion fully.

Ask yourself, 'What is this emotion about?' and when you have clarity about what the source of the emotion is, use *The Decision Tree* of Keep/Solve/Let go to work through the emotion. Once you have dealt with it fully you can resume *Supercharging*.

3. **My understanding of words like acceptance, connection, love, worthy, belonging, etc. include negative elements which pop up during *Scanning*. What do I do?**

    Everyone does not interpret the words used during *Scanning* in exactly the same way due to past experiences. You may not have a healthy reference for a word that makes up part of *Scanning*. The word 'love' for example might stir up feelings of betrayal and hurt. Check to see that you have a positive connection and connotation to all the words in your *Scan*. If you find a word that has something negative linked to it, spend some time imagining what it would be like if the word was 100% positive for you.

4. **I don't 'feel' anything when I *Scan*?**

    This can be due to mental blocks, not enough *Supercharging* energy, not using your hand and being too mentally flat.

    4.1 In order to get rid of mental blocks you need to give yourself permission to safely receive feedback from your body and your mind. This is achieved through

Supercharging and then *Scanning* using the set-up question: 'What would it mean to me if I could give myself full permission to safely receive feedback from my body and mind?'

4.2 To create more *Supercharging* energy you need to answer more 'What would it mean to me?' questions about the positive answers you are getting. Don't stop until you are smiling due to the positive energy.

4.3 Use your hand to *Scan* (open palm). It's a critical part of the technique. The most effective shape for your hand during *Scanning* is an open hand with the palm facing inwards, towards yourself with your elbow up in line with your ears.

4.4 If you are feeling mentally flat, rest and then try again when you are feeling better or after an invigorating or refreshing event (e.g. after a jog or shower).

5. **I am a sceptic and this is too weird for me – I find it very difficult to work towards growth and/or healing.**
The approach and techniques described in this book are very different to those commonly used to develop healthier self-esteem and for some people it may take them too far out of their comfort zone. But then consider this: An American high jumper named Dick Fosbury revolutionised the high jump in the late 1960's when he developed a new technique, which

became known as the 'Fosbury Flop'. The technique involves going headfirst over the bar, backward and with your body horizontal to the ground. It was and still is a very different approach when compared to the 'straddle,' or 'belly roll' which was then the high-jumping norm. His new style was heavily criticised at first and he was even called a 'lazy high jumper.' It all changed after Fosbury became a gold medallist during the 1968 Olympic Games. He revolutionised the sport and since then nearly every high jumper who took home Olympic gold has used his technique to do so.

Just like the 'Fosbury Flop' I believe *Scanning* to be a revolutionary technique. I would much rather see that you 'win gold' today, instead of waiting for the technique to become commonplace.

You can use the following *Supercharging* set-up questions to help shift your mindset:

- 'What would it mean to me if I could fully commit to this process by releasing all my doubts and blocks linked to my own growth and healing?'
- 'What would it mean to me if I could begin to find that change, growth and healing is easy and simple for me?'

6. **I don't get an answer when asking the 'What's that about?' question when I find energy in my body.**

    6.1 It could be that you don't have permission to get body feedback. If that is the case you can use the *Supercharging* set-up question, 'What would it mean to me if I could safely hear what my body is trying to tell me?'

    6.2 Check to see if the answer is delayed due to energy that is moving out of the body or being processed. You do that by focusing on the energy and asking yourself, 'Is this processing energy?'

    6.3 It will be difficult to hear the answer when you are too busy judging yourself or when you are constantly sceptical and saying, 'This won't work for me' until you are proving yourself right.

    6.4 It could be that your pain is in the way and that it needs to be addressed directly with the help of a relevant expert. You can check with the question, 'Is this pain I need expert help with?'

7. **I can't let go (of a belief) because I need to understand why I am feeling that way or why I have this belief.**

    The need to understand why you are holding on to a belief can create a block as sometimes no amount of reflection or analysis can provide an acceptable answer. My own 'need to know why' kept me stuck for many years and severely limited my healing and growth. It stopped me from moving forward. When I examined my deeper motives for wanting to know I found that I had a belief that: 'Once I truly know why I will be able to prevent this from happening ever again to me and/or my loved ones.' So even though my intentions might have been noble, it just didn't work and kept me stuck. Paradoxically letting go of 'Why' and rising above what was holding me back gave me a much better chance of preventing it from happening again.

If you do find yourself stuck in the 'Why' trap, the Permission Release statement (used instead of the normal Let go of *The Decision Tree*) to use is: 'I give myself full permission to let go of X, without having to know why. If it is actually useful to know why then I trust that my mind will reveal this information to me safely and in a way that works for me sometime in the future.'

8. **When I ask the 'What's that about?' question my memory goes blank and I associate this with a negative time in my life (when I can't remember much or anything about that time).** When there is a negative feeling linked to a blank in memory it's reasonable to assume that whatever it is that's causing the block needs to be let go of. The statement for doing that is: 'I give myself full permission to safely let go of whatever is holding me back, without having to know any details. If it's

really important to know then I trust that my mind will reveal this information to me safely and in a way that works for me when the time is right.'

9. **I can't build any *Supercharging* energy with the 'What does it mean to me?' question.**

   You may be too tired for *Scanning* to work. Get some proper rest and try again. If that's not the problem check to see whether you have permission to feel the energy linked to your meanings fully and completely. The *Scan* that will move you in the right direction has the set-up question: 'What would it mean to me if I could begin to safely feel and experience my emotions and feedback from my body?'

10. **I don't DO emotions! (I live in my own head.)**

    The result of actively and consistently ignoring or supressing emotions for a long time can be the inability to feel real emotion (both positive and negative emotions). If you can relate please note that it's a dangerous path which can lead to serious health problems in the long term. I recommend seeking out a skilled professional to work with on this. The *Supercharging* set-up question that will move you in the right direction is: 'What would it mean to me if I could begin to safely feel and experience my emotions and feedback from my body more and more?'

11. How do I work with a painful memory if and when it gets triggered by *Scanning*?

Karl Dawson is a pioneer in the healing field and has developed a powerful technique called Matrix Reimprinting which inspired some of my thinking around *Scanning*. It can be the case that during coaching or *Scanning* a specific memory of a younger you gets triggered and it needs to be dealt with directly. (This can be referred to as working with your inner child, however the memory can be of you at any age.) When that happens my recommendation of what to do changes and I base this specific approach on the guidelines and principles laid out in Karl Dawson and Kate Marillat's excellent book, *Transform your beliefs, transform your life*.

The steps to follow are below. They include a simple technique I developed when working with young athletes I call *Drop it like it's hot*. It's a release method where instead of using the words 'I give myself full permission to let this go,' you use the *feeling* of letting go and link that to what you want to let go of. I have found that especially younger clients find this method easier than the Permission Release instruction.

Drop it like it's hot: Think back to the last time you were carrying far too many heavy shopping bags. The bags were probably so heavy that your fingers began to look like pork sausages from the strain of the weight. Then recall the feeling right after you released the bags onto the kitchen counter/table or floor. That feeling of release is called *Drop it like it's hot*. Now feel that same feeling of release about something you want to let go of.... like your irritation, your fear, your worry, your feeling of not being good enough. You may have to *Drop it like it's hot* three or four times or more, and that's okay. If it helps you to flex your fingers as you 'let go' then do so. Some athletes I have worked with also practiced with their heavy sports bags to make the feeling of release as current and real as possible.

Working with the memory of the younger you:

11.1 Introduce yourself to your younger version and tell him or her that you are here to help. Dawson calls this younger version of you your ECHO.

11.2 The first thing you need to do is to ask the ECHO what he or she needs to feel safe. Your younger you might want to freeze the memory, build a wall, bring in a friend, make themselves bigger or make someone else smaller. Maybe he or she wants a big sister or brother type figure to enter the scene to tell him or her that it will 'be okay' whilst creating a protective barrier. Make sure you get the ECHO's answer to what's needed to feel safe; your adult answer is not the one we want here. You may have to make several adjustments to the memory and check in several times to make sure your ECHO is feeling safe and only once that has happened can you proceed to Step 3.

11.3 Once it is safe, ask your younger self: 'When this happened what did you decide about yourself?' Or 'What beliefs did you take on based on this experience?'

11.4 Let the younger version of yourself know that he/she doesn't have to hold onto those lies (negative beliefs), it's not true and that he/she is a good boy/girl. Teach him/her the *Drop it like it's hot* method and help them to use that or the Permission Release method to let go of the lie/limiting belief.

11.5 Check in to see if all the negatives are released. If not, ask your ECHO: 'What else do you need to let go of this?' Or 'What other things are making you unhappy?' Or 'What other negatives are you holding onto?' Use language that is age appropriate for the memory, eg. a small child's language would be simpler than a teenager's language.

11.6 Now help the younger version of you to *Scan* in the positives by first teaching *Scanning* to the ECHO and then guiding him or her through the process of locking in the most relevant beliefs of the *Game Changer Protocol*.

11.7 Once the younger version of you is in a good space, help the ECHO to spread all the positive energy around his/her entire body so that all of him/her is even more aligned with the new empowering beliefs and feelings.

11.8 Imagine that energy building up into a sonic boom wave and when it reaches its crescendo imagine a sonic boom bursting out of the younger version of yourself. It will send the updated energetic version of young you to every part of the universe (including your future self, so you get the *Back to the Future* movie effect)

12. **What do I do with a personal metaphor when it emerges during *Scanning* with no clear indication of what's needed?** Sometimes the answer to the 'What's that about question?' appears as a box ... or a mirror ... or a suitcase or any form of personal metaphor which can tell a deeper story. A personal metaphor conversation is generally a slower and longer conversation. Be patient in waiting for the answer, uncover the metaphor and work with the metaphor. One of the best guides for working with personal metaphors is a style of therapy called *Clean Language*. It's based on the work of David Grove and has been further developed by Penny Tompkins and James Lawley. Below are the five questions I use the most when working with personal metaphors.

- 'And what kind of an X is that X?' (Where X is the emerging metaphor, e.g.: 'And what kind of a box is that box?'
- 'And is there anything else about X?'

- 'And that X is like what?'
- 'And what happens next?'
- 'And what would X like to have happen?'[25]

13. How do I work with an overly-dominant internal voice/self-critic?

Your internal voice, which often becomes your internal critic, can have a powerful impact on your day to day experiences, energy and quality of life. When the internal voice/critic is dialled up too strong, you can easily begin to feel negative and drained. To dial it down and even to switch if off or to change it to a positive voice require a unique approach which I've mapped out below. This approach is also influenced by Karl Dawson's Matrix Reimprinting.

Method

13.1 Connect with one of the phrases of the internal critic and ask the question: 'What is the positive intent here?' Or 'What belief holds this phrase in place?' Most people respond quickly with: 'There is no positive intent behind this voice!' Just sit with the question for a bit and see what comes up slowly. The critic's intent is normally about safety or security. (To keep me safe/so that I don't look stupid/so that I don't make a fool of myself/so that I

---

[25] You can read more about how to work with personal metaphors at: http://www.cleanlanguage.co.uk/CleanLanguage.html

don't get judged/so that I don't do anything risky/so that I don't offend). However, it could be any positive intent. Remember, the internal critic is normally set up with a child's mind, so even if the positive intent isn't very clever or logical, it is still real and powerful.

13.2 Once you have found the positive intent behind the critic's phrase, go inside your mind and thank the critic for doing such a great job of protecting you from X (where X is the positive intent) and let the critic know: 'I don't need protection from X anymore, that role is no longer needed and is out of date.' Instead ask if you can be supported for being more Y (where Y could be more courageous, more real, more authentic, more engaging, more connected, bolder, etc.) If you can't think of something you want to be supported for when you repurpose your inner critic, then just ask it to be your genuine friend- always on your side and believing in you whilst sharing important truths kindly when relevant.

13.3 The language of step two is: 'I give myself full permission to let go using my internal voice to …… (keep me safe from making a fool of myself) and instead ask that it performs a new role for a new chapter of my life ….. (by encouraging me to engage and interact more with others in an authentic way).

13.4 If any objections or blocks come up from the Permission Release statement in step three, ask yourself, 'What is stopping me here?' Then whatever answer you get use *The Decision Tree* of Keep/Solve/Let go to work through it.

You may have to repeat this exercise several times as the internal critic triggers are normally strong and varied and there is likely to be many layers of the critic. Once you have repurposed the original layer and when a new layer comes up remind it that you are now living a new chapter of your life and what you are doing now is ......*fill in the blank, what is relevant to you*   Do this until no more layers are left.

APPENDIX A

Owning Your Power Zone

(adapted from Dr L. Michael Hall's work)

If we can take back 100% of our four personal powers, it means we can be empowered and have accountability because everything we do and say would be a personal choice and not an unwanted reaction. Building your sense of ownership about your four personal powers is called *Owning your Power Zone*.

Method

When you do the exercise for the first time, think of a time when you felt disempowered, where someone made you think something negative or feel something that negatively impacted you. Set aside that memory somewhere in your mind and then let it go for now. We will get back to it, to see how things are different once you have created your Power Zone.

Get a feel for your four personal powers: your powers of thinking, feeling, saying and doing. Notice that even the thoughts and feelings you don't like are yours. Once you own it, you can have more choice with what to do with it, including letting it go.

Recall a time when you had a strong sense of ownership about something, you may even have felt possessive over it, e.g. getting a brand new pair of shoes or a special piece of sports equipment (my racquet, my violin, my bat). Recall that moment when that thing became yours and you said to yourself: 'This is mine!'

As you recall that movie, focus on seeing what you saw, feeling what you felt and hearing what you heard, as you had that feeling of ownership, that feeling of 'Mine!' As you notice that feeling growing, see if you can double it, make it even bigger, up the intensity until it is 8 or 9 of 10 in intensity – that feeling of 'Mine!'

When you have a strong feeling of 'Mine!' - feel that about your thoughts, all of them, from the thoughts you enjoy to the ones that you don't. They are all yours. Once you own them you can manage them more effectively. Notice what that is like for you.
Now take that 'Mine!' and feel that about all of your feelings - the ones you enjoy and the ones you don't enjoy, all of them! Take ownership. Once they are yours you can start to manage them more effectively. Notice what that is like for you.

Take that feeling of 'Mine!' and feel that about all the things you say and the way you say them - your tone, your language, your ability to speak or be quiet when you need to. Notice what that is like for you.

Take that feeling of 'Mine!' and feel that about what you do, about your behaviour in every area of your life. The things you are proud of and not so proud of. Notice what that is like for you.

Wrap up

Access your strong feeling of 'Mine!' and feel that about your thinking, feeling, saying and doing. Notice what it's like for you when you have a stronger sense of owning all four of your powers - what it is like to feel that empowered. Now with this strong sense of empowerment, recall that time when you were disempowered from earlier and see how things are now different. Take a moment to think about future events where you would benefit from accessing your Power Zone and what that will be like NOW.

APPENDIX B

Heart Breathing

(source: HeartMath Institute)

1. Sit upright in your chair, get comfortable and close your eyes.
2. Put your hand over your heart and focus your attention on that area – on the deep chambers in the centre of your chest.
3. Breathe deeply but normally and imagine that your breath coming in and out of your heart area.
4. Begin to regulate your breathing to a count of six.
5. Breathe for a count of six seconds into your heart space.
6. Breathe for a count of six seconds out of your heart space.
7. Keep breathing in for six and breathing out for six.
8. Repeat breathing into the heart area for a count of six and out of the heart area for a count of six for several minutes until you find yourself at the level of calm that works for you.

Optional extra

As you breathe out, imagine breathing out any or all negativity with that breath. Breathe out your frustration, anger and stress.

Bibliography

Bókkon, I., Salari, V., Tuszynski, J. and Antal, I. (2010) *Estimation of the number of biophotons involved in the visual perception of a single-object image: Biophoton intensity can be considerably higher inside cells than outside*, Journal of photochemistry and photobiology. B, Biology., 100(3), pp. 160–6.
http://www.ncbi.nlm.nih.gov/pubmed/20584615
(Accessed 12 June 2016).

Branden, N. (1995) *The six pillars of self-esteem*. New York, NY: Random House Publishing Group.

Brown, B.C. (2010) Brené Brown: *The power of vulnerability*. [video] Available at:
http://www.ted.com/talks/Brené_brown_on_vulnerability.html
(Accessed 12 June 2016).

Brown, B.C. (2010) *The gifts of imperfection: Let go of who you think you're supposed to be and embrace who you are*. United States: Hazelden Information & Educational Services.

Brown, B (2012) *Brené Brown: Listening to Shame*. [video] Available at:
http://www.ted.com/talks/Brené_brown_listening_to_shame.html
(Accessed: 12 June 2016).

Brown, B. (2012). *Daring greatly: how the courage to be vulnerable transforms the way we live, love, parent, and lead*.
New York, NY, Gotham Books.

Brown, B. (2015) *Rising Strong*. United States: Spiegel & Grau

Brown, J. D., & Marshall, M. A. (2006) *The three faces of self-esteem*. Available at:
http://faculty.washington.edu/jdb/448/448articles/kernis.pdf
(Accessed: 12 June 2016).

Chau, C. *'I'm a Fraud' – What to Do When You Have the Impostor Syndrome*. Available at: http://personalexcellence.co/blog/impostor-syndrome/ (Accessed: 12 June 2016).

Cooper, M. and Goodenough, T. (2007) *In the zone with South Africa's sports heroes: How to achieve top performance in sport and life*. South Africa: Zebra Press.

Cuddy, A. (2015) *Presence: Bringing your boldest self to your biggest challenges*. United States: Little Brown and Company.

Dawson, K. and Allenby, S. (2010) *Matrix Reimprinting using EFT: Rewrite your past, transform your future*. United Kingdom: Hay House UK.

Dawson, K. Marillat, K. (2014) *Transform your beliefs transform your life*. United Kingdom: Hay House UK.

Dotta, B., Saroka, K. and Persinger, M. (2012) *Increased photon emission from the head while imagining light in the dark is correlated with changes in electroencephalographic power: Support for Bókkon's biophoton hypothesis, Neuroscience letters.*, 513(2), pp. 151–4. http://www.ncbi.nlm.nih.gov/pubmed/22343311 (Accessed: 12 June 2016).

Dweck, C.S. (2006) *Mindset: The new psychology of success*. New York: Random House Publishing Group.

Ferriss, T. (2010) *The 4-hour body: An uncommon guide to rapid fat-loss, incredible sex, and becoming superhuman*. New York: Crown Publishing Group.

Ferriss, T. (2015) *Brené Brown on vulnerability and home run TED talks*. Available at: http://fourhourworkweek.com/2015/08/28/brene-brown-on-vulnerability-and-home-run-ted-talks/ (Accessed: 12 June 2016).

Goodenough, T. and Cooper, M. (2012) *Raising talent: How to fast-track potential into performance*. South Africa: The Penguin Group (SA) (Pty).

Grant, A.M. (2014) *Give and take: Why helping others drives our success*. United States: Penguin Books.

Hall, Dr L.M. (2011) *Neuro-Semantics: Actualizing meaning and performance*. Clifton: Neuro-Semantic Publications.

Hamilton, D.R (2015) *I heart me: The science of self-love*. United Kingdom: Hay House UK.

Holiday, R. (2016) *Ego is the enemy*. United States: Portfolio.

Institute, H. (2012) *Heart-focused breathing - HeartMath institute*. Available at: https://www.heartmath.org/articles-of-the-heart/the-math-of-heartmath/heart-focused-breathing/
(Accessed: 12 June 2016).

Ji, S. (2013) *Biophotons: The Human Body Emits, Communicates with and is Made from Light*. Available at: http://www.greenmedinfo.com/blog/biophotons-human-body-emits-communicates-and-made-light (Accessed: 12 June 2016).

King, S. (2015) *Heal your birth, heal your life: Tools to transform your birth experience and create a magical new beginning*. United Kingdom: SilverWood Books.

Lipton, B. (2011) *The Biology of Belief: Unleashing the Power of Consciousness, Matter & Miracles*. London: Hay House.

Loyd, A. and Johnson, B. (2011) *The healing code: 6 minutes to heal the source of your health, success or relationship issue*. United Kingdom: Hodder & Stoughton General Division

Loyd, A. (2015) *Beyond Willpower: The secret principle to achieving success in life, love and happiness*. London: Yellow Kite.

Moorjani, A. and Dyer, W.W. (2012) *Dying to be me: My journey from cancer, to near death, to true healing*.

Carlsbad, CA: Hay House.

Pert, C. and Pert, ace (2004) *Your body is your subconscious mind.* United States: Sounds True.

Strauss, N. (2015) *The truth: An uncomfortable book about relationships.* United States: Dey Street Books.

Strauss, N. (2015) *What I learned about relationships after cheating on my wife.* Available at: http://www.telegraph.co.uk/wellbeing/mood-and-mind/neil-strauss-truth-childhood-relationships-marriage-dating-problem-parents-family-advice/ (Accessed: 12 June 2016).

Wilkinson, C. (2013) *Dad - the power and beauty of authentic Fatherhood.* United States: Dad Books.

Wilkinson, C. (2015) *Real man, real dad.* [video] Available at: https://www.youtube.com/watch?v=4NGRw71RBOU (Accessed: 12 June 2016).

www.ingramcontent.com/pod-product-compliance
Lightning Source LLC
Chambersburg PA
CBHW051403290426
44108CB00015B/2134